Introduction

Creating a successful design these days often requires just as much technical knowledge as it does creativity: *Quark Design* wraps both of these elements into one package: In this book you'll find hundreds of ideas for creating stunning, effective designs. In the process, you'll learn the actual steps taken by designers to execute their ideas in QuarkXPress, with hints and tips on how to get from concept to printed materials via the most efficient route.

There are no rules on how to use this book. You can read it from start to finish if you like, or you can jump from page to page, stopping to look at the designs that catch your eye or to read about the type of publications that interest you. The icons preceding italicized type indicate a tip: A magnifying glass 🔍 signifies technical information, while a painter's palette 🎨 signifies design information.

The first part of this book offers an overview of QuarkXPress. Some of the material is pretty basic, but you'll also find nuggets of technical information that you might not have known about, even if you're a QuarkXPress power user.

The second section, which comprises the bulk of this book, contains step-by-step examples of documents created in QuarkXPress. Sometimes you'll see the creation of a project from start to finish; other times I'll focus on one particular aspect of a design that was especially useful, beautiful, or just plain interesting. Either way, you can get a feel for the progression of a QuarkXPress document just by looking at the pictures. You won't want to skip the captions however, as you'll glean some valuable information from those, too.

The third section focuses on workgroup publishing tools. Even those of us who work from home know that publishing does not happen in a vacuum. Collaboration between writers, editors, art directors, designers, and production managers is even more challenging in the age of personal computers. I've taken the opportunity to highlight some of the software tools available today that enable QuarkXPress users to work together more cohesively and more efficiently.

I've also devoted a chapter to showcasing some QuarkXPress XTensions, those wonderful little software programs that let us customize and add functionality to QuarkXPress. There was no way I could depict all of the available XTensions, so I took the liberty of choosing a few that are particularly applicable to designers and production personnel.

I hope you learn a lot about QuarkXPress from this book. I also hope you find it inspirational from a creative standpoint. I know that I was inspired by all of the wonderful design work I came across while researching, writing, and producing this book.

—*Nancy J. McCarthy*

Contents

Chapter One: QuarkXPress Basics

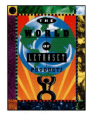

Chapter Two: Magazine Design

Chapter Three: Advertising Design

Chapter Four: Booklets

Chapter Five: Identities

Chapter Six: Catalogs

Chapter Seven: Brochures

QUARK DESIGN

A STEP-BY-STEP APPROACH TO PAGE LAYOUT SOFTWARE

BY NANCY J. McCARTHY

PEACHPIT PRESS

Quark Design
Nancy J. McCarthy

Peachpit Press
2414 Sixth Street
Berkeley, CA 94710
(510) 548-4393
(510) 548-5991 (fax)

Peachpit Press is a division of Addison-Wesley Publishing Company.

Cover design: Kristin FitzGerrell
Interior design: Nancy Rice
Art director: Nancy McCarthy
Technical editor: Jeff Cheney
Production: Rainwater Press

This book is typeset in Monotype Janson, Monotype Janson Expert, and Futura Extra Bold. The display type on the front and back covers is Copperplate from Adobe Systems Inc. and Grizzly from Image Club Graphics. The picture fonts used within the body text are from Letraset USA's Fontek DesignFonts Organics collection.

ISBN 0-201-88376-7

9 8 7 6 5 4 3 2 1
Printed in Hong Kong

Dedication

To Pat, Ben, and Cole

Acknowledgments

I would first like to thank all of the designers featured in this book who shared with me their time, their expertise, and their artwork. This book is a showcase of their talent. Their names and addresses are listed in the back of the book.

Many people had a direct impact on the creation of this book, and I would like to thank them: Kristin FitzGerrell, for her designs of the front and back covers; Nancy Rice, for her design of the interior page templates; Kristy Astry, for her assistance in the initial stages of production; and Jeff Cheney, for his expert advice as my technical editor.

Warm thanks also go to Eric Jacobs of *The Daily Pennsylvanian*, Edward Renaud of St. Remy Press, and Dennis McGuire and Peter Kelts of Managing Editor Software, for their assistance in creating the chapter on workgroup publishing; and to Chris Ryland of Em Software, Larry McMunn of McMunn Associates, and Bill Buckingham and Jim Wiegand of XChange, for their assistance in creating the chapter on Quark XPress XTensions.

I would also like to thank those people who contributed to this book in an indirect, though no less important way, by offering their advice, technical assistance, and moral support: Linnea Dayton, Joel Sironen, David Ambler, Wayne Sirmons, Kevin Hambel, Kass Johns, David Blatner, Steve Roth, and Kathleen Tinkel, for her unwavering support throughout my career in this industry.

And finally, I would like to thank my husband Patrick, who read every page of this book as it came out of my laser printer; my two sons Ben and Cole, for giving me the most important job of a lifetime; my sister Gerarda, for her friendship; my father in-law Bob McCarthy, for his genuine interest in my career; and my mom, for being proud of me even though she still can't figure out what it is I do for a living.

Nancy J. McCarthy, May 1995.

QuarkXPress Basics

QUARKXPRESS

A VISUAL GUIDE FOR THE MAC

A STEP-BY-STEP APPROACH TO LEARNING PAGE LAYOUT SOFTWARE

BLACKCAT   BLACKCAT   BLACKCAT

BY NANCY J. McCARTHY

QuarkXPress is a complex program. This chapter serves merely as an overview of QuarkXPress' intricate structure and powerful capabilities. It will help you understand the basic logic behind the program and to familiarize yourself with its major tools. In going over the basics, we'll show you how designers Kristin FitzGerrell and Nancy Rice created the covers and page templates for this book.

The cover design shown here and in the following pages appears on the international versions of Quark Design.

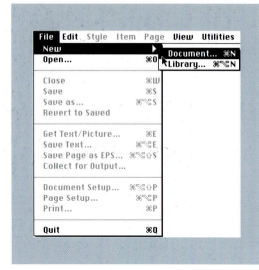

Starting from scratch

1. When you first launch QuarkXPress, you have three choices under the File menu: Create a new document, open an existing document, or quit the program. *In versions 3.2 and later, you also have the option to create a new Library from the File menu.*

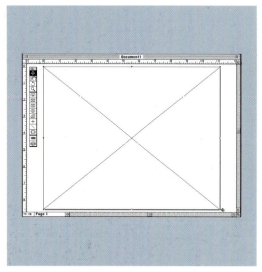

6. FitzGerrell used the rectangular picture box tool to draw her first picture box, which would encompass the entire width and height of her new document.

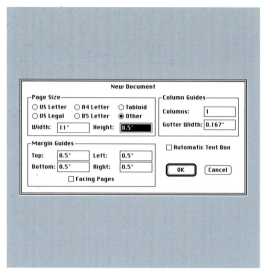

2. If you're creating a completely new design instead of revising an existing one, select New Document from the File menu. Because our book cover would be landscape instead of portrait orientation, FitzGerrell specified the dimensions of her new document as 11 inches wide by 8.5 inches high.

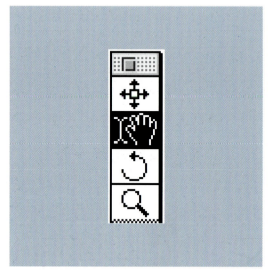

Tools for editing

7. The four tools at the top of the Tool palette are for moving, adjusting, rotating, and viewing boxes and items within boxes that you have already created. The item tool (top) lets you manipulate text boxes, picture boxes, and lines; the content tool (second from top) lets you manipulate items *within* text and picture boxes.

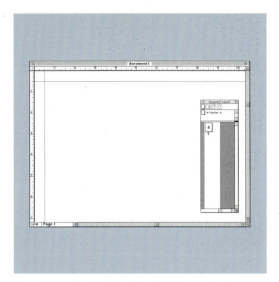

3. After specifying the basic characteristics of your new document, you now have an empty page shown at Actual Size, or 100%. Unlike many other programs, you cannot begin placing text or graphics on your QuarkXPress page until you have first created a text box or a picture box.

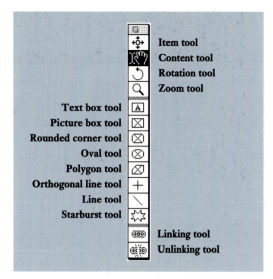

Item tool
Content tool
Rotation tool
Zoom tool
Text box tool
Picture box tool
Rounded corner tool
Oval tool
Polygon tool
Orthogonal line tool
Line tool
Starburst tool
Linking tool
Unlinking tool

The Tool palette

4. Before proceeding any further, you should be familiar with the basic function of each of the tools within the QuarkXPress Tool palette. Think of it as your home base, where you will return (using the mouse or keyboard shortcuts) each time you want to create a new item or change an existing one.

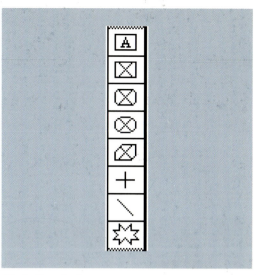

Tools for creating

5. The items in the middle of the Tool palette are for creating text boxes, picture boxes, and lines. *To navigate down the Tool palette without using the mouse, press Command Tab. To move up the Tool palette, press Command Shift Tab.*

8. The rotation tool (third from top on the Tool palette) lets you manually rotate text and picture boxes from 360 to minus 360 degrees. *When using the rotation tool to rotate a text or a picture box, click on the rotation axis to select it, then drag away from it to create a "lever" before rotating.*

9. The zoom tool (fourth from top on the Tool palette) lets you view objects up to 400 times their actual size. *An easy way to zoom in on an area is to click and drag across the item using the zoom tool—XPress will automatically fill your screen with the area you have selected. You can temporarily change the content tool or item tool into the zoom tool by holding down the Control key.*

Linking and unlinking tools

10. To link two text boxes, select the linking tool, click on a text box, then click on an empty text box. *When your text runs across more than one text box or page, link the text boxes together so that when changes are made, the text stays together in one continuous flow.*

The Measurements palette

11. The Measurements palette can be used to modify text and pictures, lines, and groups of items; it will look different depending on what type of item is selected. This picture shows the Measurements palette when a text box has been selected. *Press Command Option M to display the Measurements palette.*

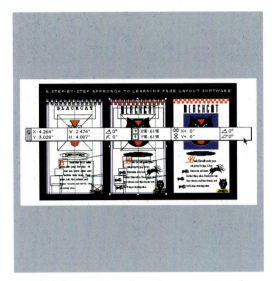

12. The left side of the palette always contains information pertaining to a selected item, while the right side of the palette contains information regarding the *contents* of that item. This picture shows the Measurements palette when a picture box has been selected. *Press Return or Enter to apply any new values you've typed into the Measurements palette.*

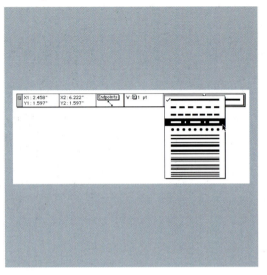

13. Here's what the Measurements palette looks like when a line is selected, showing the different types of lines that can be automatically created in XPress. You can navigate through the Measurements palette using the Tab key. *The Measurements palette will show informaton on the contents of an item only when the content tool is selected.*

The Colors palette

17. You can use the Colors palette to apply colors to text, pictures, boxes, lines, and frames and to specify one- and two-color blends. *A quick way to add color to a box is to simply click on the colored square in the palette, drag, and drop it into a text or picture box.*

Specifying blends

18. To specify the circular blend that appears in the chapter openers for this book, designer Nancy Rice selected the picture box that would contain the blend, selected Circular Blend from the Blend pop-up menu, and selected Light Tan from the Colors palette.

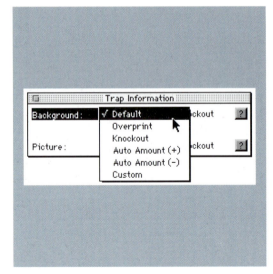

The Trap Information palette

19. This palette lets you override default trapping settings on an item-by-item basis; it also lets you specify custom trapping values. *Be sure to discuss any trapping issues you may have regarding your design with your printer before you go on press.*

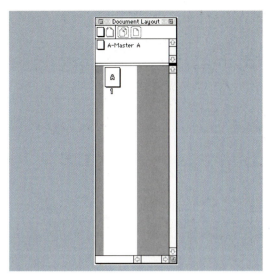

The Document Layout palette

14. This palette provides a handy way to create, modify, and apply master pages, and to insert, delete, and move document pages without going through the Page menu. It's especially useful when navigating through a multi-page document: Simply double-click on the page icon you wish to view.

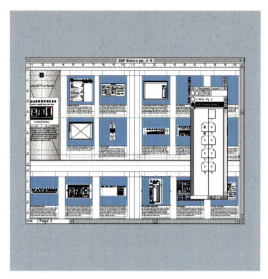

Inserting pages

15. To easily insert pages into your document, use the Document Layout palette by clicking on a blank page icon (top of palette) or a master page icon (second row of palette) and dragging it into the palette. We added four master pages to this section of the book by clicking and dragging one of the master page icons.

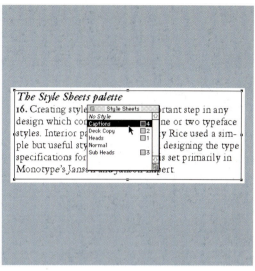

The Style Sheets palette

16. Creating style sheets is an important step in any design that contains more than one or two typeface styles. Interior page designer Nancy Rice used a simple but useful style sheet system in designing the type specifications for this book, which is set primarily in Monotype's Janson and Janson Expert.

The Library palette

20. You can store frequently used text and graphics in the Library palette. To store an item, simply select it with the Item tool and drag it to the Library palette. To copy an item, drag it from the Library palette into your document. QuarkXPress creates a duplicate of the item and leaves the original intact.

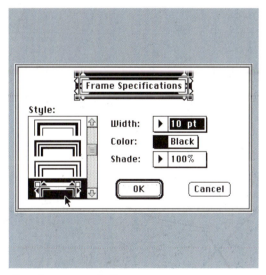

Creating automatic frames

21. XPress offers several styles of frames that you can use to automatically frame a picture box or a text box. Frames that are chosen from the Frame Specifications dialog box under the Item menu can be colorized and shaded. ☀ *You can also create custom frames using the Frame Editor, but these will be bitmapped (not PostScript).*

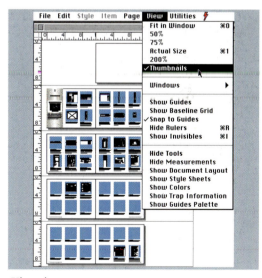

View sizes

22. You can view your XPress pages in a variety of sizes (including Thumbnails, shown above) using the View menu or the percentage field in the lower left corner of the XPress window. ☀ *Press Control V to automatically highlight the percentage field.*

Importing text

23. FitzGerrell used the Get Text command to import the back cover copy from a Microsoft Word document. ☀: *Depending on whether you have a text box or a picture box selected, you'll find "Get Text" or "Get Picture" under the File menu.*

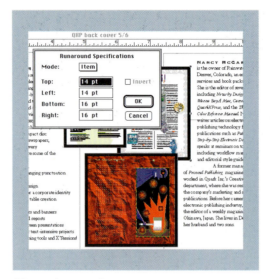

Text wraparounds

24. To create the automatic text wraparounds on the back cover, FitzGerrell entered the amount of space she wanted at the top, left, bottom, and right of the selected image in the Runaround Specifications dialog under the Item menu. ☀: *Use "Manual Image" when you want to create irregularly shaped text wraps.*

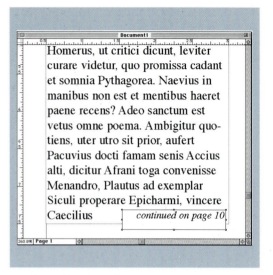

Implementing jump lines

25. If you're creating a magazine or newsletter in which text is linked between non-consecutive pages, you can use the Next Box Page Number and Previous Box Page Number commands to insert jump lines. ☀: *Press Command 4 for Next Box ("continued on") and Command 2 for Previous Box ("continued from").*

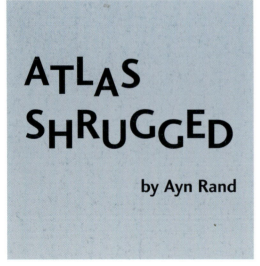

Baseline shift

29. QuarkXPress' Baseline Shift command lets you move characters above or below the baseline to achieve some interesting headline effects. ☀: *Press Command Option Shift - (hyphen) to lower selected type, and Command Option Shift + (plus) to raise it.*

Kerning

30. To kern (adjust the spacing between two letters) in XPress, place the text cursor between the two letters you wish to kern, and click the right or left arrow in the Measurements palette. Notice the spacing between the "R" and the "A" in the example without kerning (top) and with kerning (bottom).

Tracking

31. You can track text (adjust the overall spacing between several letters) using the same tools used for kerning: Highlight the characters you wish to track and click the right or left arrow in the Measurements palette. ☀: *Hold down the Option key while clicking the arrows to track in smaller increments.*

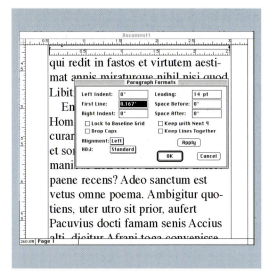

Indenting paragraphs

26. If you've been indenting paragraphs using the Tab key, there's still hope for you. The Paragraph Formats dialog box under the Style menu lets you automatically apply indents to the first line of paragraphs, among other things. ☀: *Command Shift F is the keyboard shortcut for the Paragraph Formats dialog.*

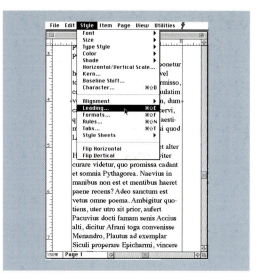

Applying leading

27. You can adjust leading (the distance from baseline to baseline) through the Leading dialog box under the Style menu or via the Measurements palette. ☀: *Press Command Shift ' (apostrophe) to increase leading or Command Shift ; (semicolon) to decrease leading in 1-pt. increments within a selected text box.*

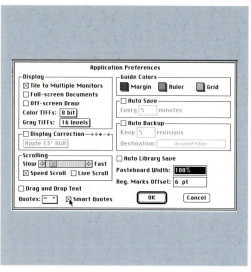

Using typographer's quotes

28. QuarkXPress will convert all of your quote marks to typographer's quotes (also known as curly quotes) if you check the Smart Quotes option in the Application Preferences dialog under the Edit menu. ☀: *If you need to type inch and foot marks when Smart Quotes is on, press Control ' or Control Shift ".*

All that is told here happened some time before Mowgli was turned out of the Seeonee Wolf Pack, or revenged himself on Shere Khan the Tiger. It was in the days when Baloo was teaching him the Law of the Jungle. The big, serious, old brown bear was delighted to have so quick a pupil, for the young wolves will only learn as much of the Law of the Jungle as applies to their own pack and tribe, and run away as soon as they can repeat the Hunting Verse.

Creating automatic drop caps

32. The Paragraph Formats dialog box lets you easily specify automatic drop caps by entering the number of characters that will be dropped, and the number of lines the letters will occupy. The above example shows one character dropped two lines.

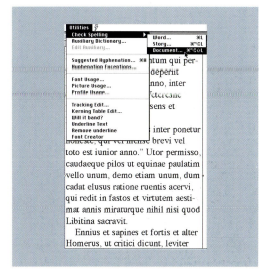

Spell-checking your documents

33. Although the QuarkXPress spelling checker is not as thorough as a dedicated spell checker and a human proofreader, it's still a good idea to use it as a first pass through your pages. You can check the spelling of a word, a story, or an entire document by selecting Check Spelling under the Utilities menu.

Font Usage dialog

34. The Font Usage dialog box under the Utilities menu is a great way to see a list of all the fonts used in your document. It's also useful for performing search-and-replace functions by font, style, and point size.

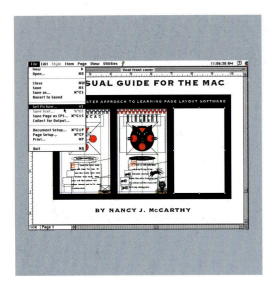

Importing pictures

35. You can import a variety of graphic file formats, including EPS, PICT, TIFF, and Kodak Photo CD images, into QuarkXPress using the Get Picture command under the File menu. ☀: *Command E will also give you the Get Picture dialog when a picture box is selected with the content tool.*

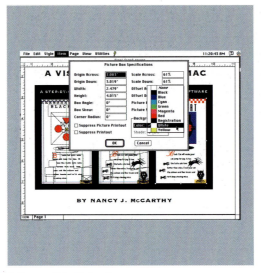

The Modify dialog box

36. Once you've imported a picture into XPress, the Modify dialog under the Item menu will let you resize, rotate, reposition, skew, and specify background colors and shades for picture boxes or their contents, depending on whether the Item or the Content tool is selected.

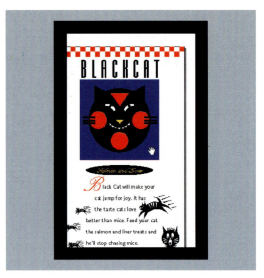

Moving picture boxes vs. moving contents

37. When working with graphics, you can move a graphic within a picture box by using the Grabber hand (Content tool); or you can move the entire picture box, including its contents, using the Item tool. ☀: *Press the Command key to temporarily turn the Content tool into the Item tool.*

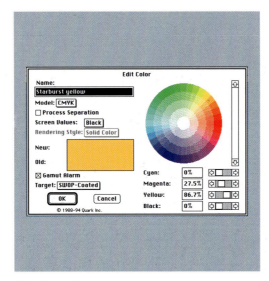

Step and Repeat

41. Using the Step and Repeat command under the Item menu will save loads of time if you need to duplicate an item more than once. Super Step and Repeat (shown above and available with Quark's free Bobzilla XTension) offers even more options.

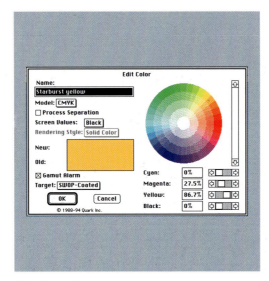

Creating colors

42. The Colors command under the Edit menu lets you create new colors and edit existing colors (above), according to a variety of color models and matching systems, including CMYK, RGB, HSB, Pantone®, and Toyo. ☀: *Command-click on a color name in the Colors palette to open the Edit Color dialog.*

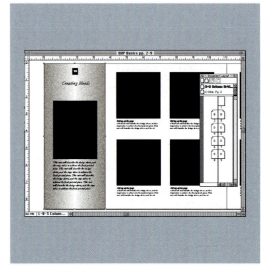

Creating bleeds

43. Designer Nancy Rice simply positioned the left hand picture box so that it extended 1/8-inch beyond the top, left, and bottom edges of the page (partially resting on the QuarkXPress pasteboard) to create the bleed for the opening chapters of this book.

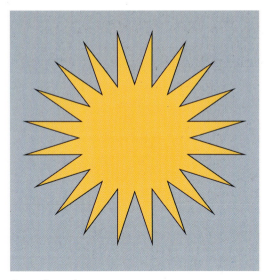

Irregular polygons

38. Though they don't seem to have much use in high-end publishing, you can create lots of neat shapes using the polygon picture box tools provided by the Box Shape submenu under the Item menu. *You can press Command-period to delete a polygon before you've finished drawing it.*

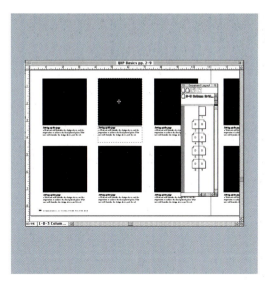

Grouping and ungrouping items

39. To group two or more items in XPress, hold down the Shift key as you select each item to be grouped, then press Command G. Designer Nancy Rice grouped each picture box with its caption as she designed the interior pages of this book. To ungroup selected grouped items, press Command U.

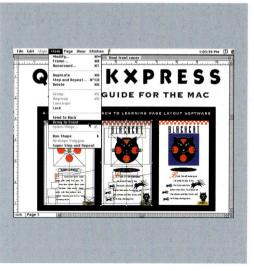

Send to Back and Bring to Front commands

40. You can have multiple layers of items in XPress; the Send to Back and Bring to Front commands let you move selected items to the back or to the fore-front of several items. *Press the Option key while selecting Send to Back or Send to Front to move items layer by layer.*

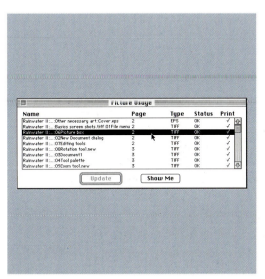

Picture Usage dialog

44. The Picture Usage dialog box under the Utilities menu is a great way to check the status of all of the graphics used in your design before getting ready to send your files to a service bureau. It will tell you if any pictures are missing and provide you with the opportunity to update them on-the-fly.

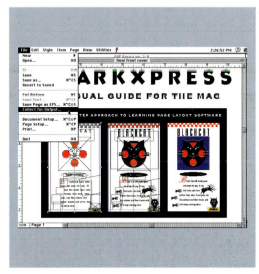

Collect for Output

45. Before you send your QuarkXPress document to a service bureau for high-resolution output, it's a good idea to perform a Collect for Output (under the File menu) in order to generate a report of all the fonts and picture files you've used in your design.

Output Request form

46. You can either print out the Collect for Output report as is, or use the Output Request template included with QuarkXPress. Fill out the template and import your report into the text box at the bottom of the page. Your service bureau will love you!

Designing a Table of Contents

Kevin P. Hambel

The pages for this two-page Table of Contents appear back-to-back in IHS Publishing's Surface Mount Technology Magazine. *Art Director Kevin Hambel made use of some stunning typographic effects such as QuarkXPress' Paragraph Rules in addition to scanned photographs, line art, and a twelve-column grid to add continuity and pizazz to his pages.*

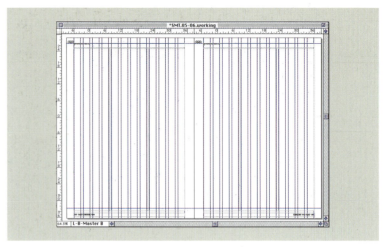

Starting with a grid

1. Hambel uses a twelve-column grid for the design of the entire magazine, which allows him a great amount of freedom yet also helps him to maintain a consistent look throughout the publication. He developed the above twelve-column grid based upon the ad sizes for *Surface Mount Technology*, so that he can position a variety of different-size elements without changing the grid. The grid also lets him size and position design elements and columns of text quickly and easily with mathematical precision. ✂ *Using a grid will give your designs a look of overall cleanliness, and need not constrain your imagination.*

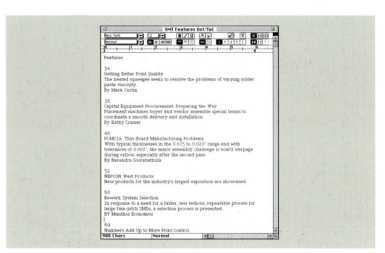

Laying the groundwork for the magazine's contents

4. At the same time Hambel's production staff is working on the template, *SMT*'s editorial staff has begun to outline the articles that will run that month, along with approximate page counts and a prioritization of the stories. As the issue unfolds, the editors have created a Microsoft Word file (above) in plain text with carriage returns after page numbers, titles, deck copy, and bylines. It's necessary to have carriage returns after each new style, because you can't have character-based styles in XPress—only paragraph-based styles.

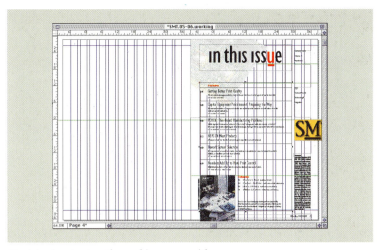

Positioning text and graphics on a grid

2. Here you can see how Art Director Kevin Hambel combines creativity with order when placing text and graphics on the first page of *SMT*'s Table of Contents. Some of the design elements are neatly placed within two, three, and four columns of the grid, while other elements (the ghosted circuit board in the upper left corner for example) break away from the grid to add visual impact. Hambel created this twelve-column grid by specifying twelve columns in the New Document dialog box when he originally set up his master pages.

Starting with a clean template

3. It's tempting to simply copy over the previous issue's Table of Contents page and start working from there, but Hambel says there's too great a chance for errors with that method. Instead, he has set up a routine in which *SMT*'s production staff is instructed to start with a clean template (left) that includes only those items that appear from issue to issue such as the headline and subscription and copyright information. The staff then follows a list of items which are manually updated, such as the date of the publication and the issue number (right) in addition to the page numbers.

Assigning and adding styles

5. Hambel eventually hopes to have the typographic styles applied to the text before it reaches his department, but for now it arrives at the art department with no styles. He uses an extensive style sheet system for *SMT* that includes the variety of type styles in the Table of Contents as well as those used in feature articles and departments. Most of the styles have a numeric keypad equivalent, which Hambel assigned using the Edit Style Sheets dialog box found via the Edit menu's Style Sheets command (above).

Flowing in the text

6. The Word documents supplied by the editors are flowed into the Quark XPress template and formatted using the numeric keypad "in a matter of 15 seconds," according to Hambel.

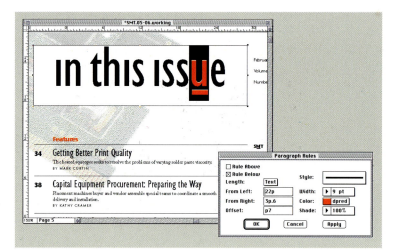

Rules above

7. Also included in Hambel's style sheets are Paragraph Rules. For example, when a page number is formatted in the Table of Contents, a black hairline rule is automatically attached above it (left) using XPress' Rule Above feature. Hambel tries to specify as many rules as possible via the Style Sheets palette so he doesn't have to spend time manually creating them. *Command Shift N will bring up the Paragraph Rules dialog box (right).*

Rules below

8. The Table of Contents headline includes a 9-pt. red Rule Below the letter "U." Applying rules to text via the Paragraph Rules dialog box is not only quicker and easier than using the Line tools, it keeps the rule anchored to the paragraph even if the paragraph is moved. In addition, using the Rule Below command allows many more typographic options than simply using the Underline style. Hambel specified the Rule Below (shown above) in order to continue a theme that was established with the logo (step 9).

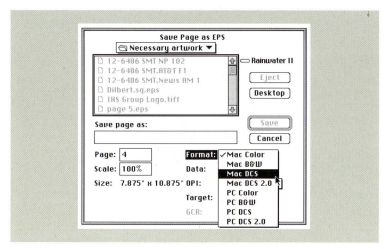

Adding graphics

11. Hambel uses EPS images such as the ghosted circuit board in the background of the first Table of Contents page to keep the technology theme forefront in the reader's mind. Most of *SMT*'s graphic images are saved in the five-file DCS (Desktop Color Separation) format, which includes four CMYK separations (Cyan, Magenta, Yellow, and Black) plus a PICT file for previewing.

Creating DCS files

12. You can color separate your QuarkXPress pages before sending them to the printer using one of two DCS formats: DCS 2.0 places your color separations all in one file and has the ability to include spot color plates; or DCS 1.0, which produces the five-file format that Hambel uses. *Although you can create DCS files via XPress' Save Page as EPS dialog (above), you have more control over the separations if you create them in a color retouching program such as Photoshop.*

Using a rule below in a logo

9. The icon Hambel shows on the Table of Contents page (above) is a representation of the magazine's cover logo. The underline below the letter "M" is an integral part of the design. According to Hambel, *Surface Mount Technology*'s original logo also featured an underline, below the words "Surface Mount." When Hambel and his assistant art director Lisa Lappe redesigned the logo, their aim was to maintain some of its visual aspects. They continue this look throughout the rest of the magazine by underlining letters within department heads and the like.

Positioning the logo on the Contents pages

10. Hambel used the *SMT* logo icon to achieve a variety of design purposes. Using the front of the logo on the first Contents page (left) signifies the front section of the magazine such as feature articles and columns, while using the end of the logo on the second Contents page (right) signifies the back matter of the book such as departments and new products. Furthermore, Hambel positioned the icon exactly where the reader's thumb would be placed when flipping through the publication. This strategic use of positioning icon-like page identifiers is used throughout *Surface Mount Technology*.

Photographic images

13. Because most of *SMT*'s photos are supplied by industry vendors, Hambel and his staff perform a large amount of electronic manipulation to clean them up or make them more dramatic. The above photograph was outlined in Adobe Photoshop to eliminate a dark background. Hambel uses much of the same artwork that appears in the feature articles and departments to add graphic interest to the Table of Contents pages. The photographs are scanned once by Hambel's service bureau, and the same scan is used throughout the magazine.

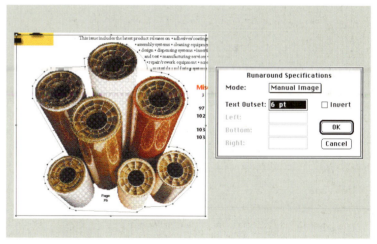

Text wraparounds

14. Here you can see how Hambel created a Manual Image runaround to wrap the text around the graphic image in the New Products section of the Contents page. When he selected "Manual Image" in the Runaround Specifications dialog (under the Item menu), a second set of handles, called the Runaround polygon, appeared (above left). Hambel then manipulated the handles so the text would wrap to his liking. ☼ *You can add and delete points along the runaround polygon by Command-clicking on a segment or existing point, respectively.*

Coloring and Layering Type

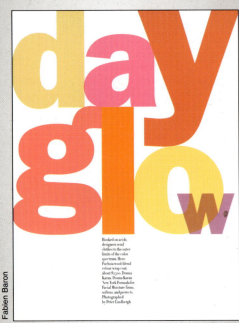

Fabien Baron

Creative Director Fabien Baron shares techniques on how he colors and layers type in QuarkXPress to make a headline into a work of art for Hearst Magazine's Harper's Bazaar.

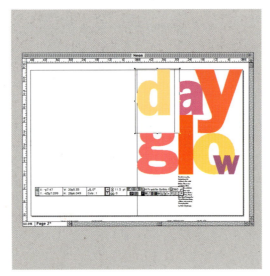

Breaking away from a grid

1. Although the pages of *Harper's Bazaar* are based on a fairly loose grid, many of the fashion spreads break away from the grid entirely. Fabien created this headline for a feature on neon clothing, with the opening caption, "Hot pink. Rocket red. Lime green. Designers send clothes to the outer limits of the color spectrum."

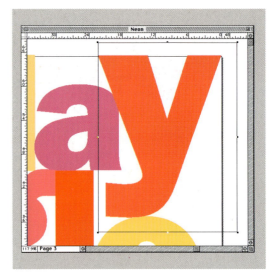

Placing letters in individual text boxes

2. As you can see from the above screen shots, Fabien placed each letter in its own text box, moving it around the page like a piece of a puzzle. Here you can see the "Y" as he positioned it to bleed off the upper right corner of the page.

Creating letters out of geometric shapes

4. This looks like a lowercase "L," but it is actually a colored text box that Fabien created to look like an "l." XPress won't let you size a text box smaller than the bounding box of the type, as it appears to do so above.

Coloring type and text boxes

5. After drawing the rectangular text box, Fabien simply applied the bright orange color via the Colors palette. He colorized the rest of the type in much the same manner, selecting each individual letter and applying a color from the palette.

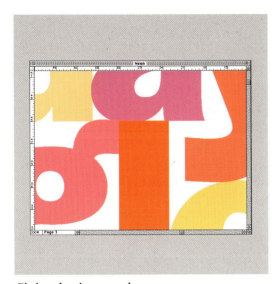

Fitting the pieces together

3. Here's a closeup of the XPress page shown at 200%, where you can see how carefully Fabien arranged the tops and bottoms of the letters against each other. Hearst's color separator takes care of the trapping and other prepress issues so that Fabien can focus on the creative aspect of the design.

Specifying a variety of point sizes

6. Set in Franklin Gothic Heavy, the "w" is the smallest of the type, set at 200 pts. The "d" is 360 pts.; the "a" is 350 pts.; and the "y" is 500 pts.; while the "g" is 400 pts. and the "o" is 418 pts. ☼: *To resize type using the keyboard, hold down Command Option Shift and press ">" to enlarge text or "<" to reduce it in 1-pt increments.*

Working with large type

7. Fabien likes to work with type in large point sizes and wishes that he could work with even bigger type in QuarkXPress. (The point size limit in XPress is 720 points.) Here's the "g" used in the Day Glow headline at actual size. Although he believes XPress is "perfect for modern magazine design," Fabien would like to see the XPress pasteboard enlarged so that he has more freedom to move his letters on and off the page while experimenting with type.

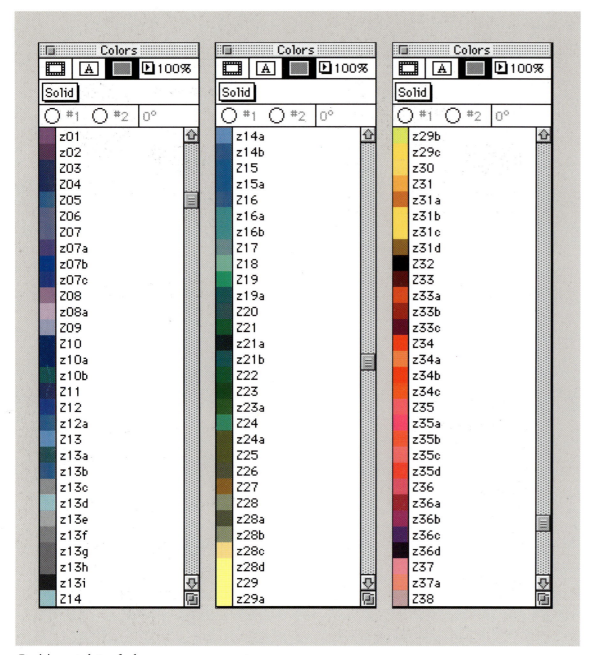

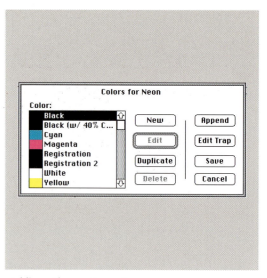

Adding other custom colors
9. In addition to the CMYK custom colors and the standard colors included in the XPress Colors palette, the *Harper's Bazaar* colors also include a second black, featuring 40% Cyan.

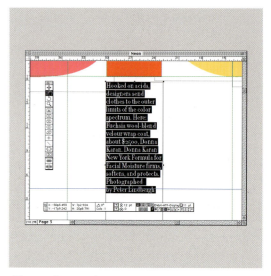

Typesetting captions
13. Most of the captions in the fashion spreads are set in a custom version of Didot (above), created exclusively for *Harper's Bazaar* by Jonathan Hoefler of the Hoefler Type Foundry in New York.

Devising a palette of colors
8. Fabien and his crew have devised an entire color scheme to be used on all of the pages of *Harper's Bazaar*, ranging from cool to warm tones. Above you can see the CMYK colors as they appear in the XPress Colors palette. Though the colors were selected to match Pantone colors, the numbering scheme does not reflect Pantone equivalents.

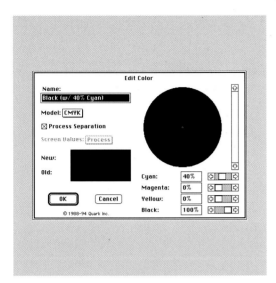

10. Created using the Edit Colors dialog box (above), the "Black (w/ 40% cyan)" is used when an extra-rich black is needed, on a black page or in a black background, for example.

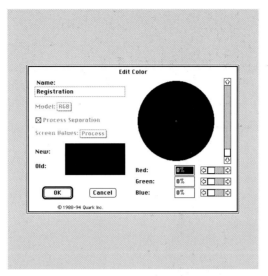

11. The XPress Colors palette at *Bazaar* also features two Registration blacks: The standard XPress Registration, above, which is comprised of 0% Red, Green, and Blue (RGB), and…

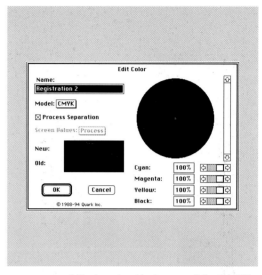

12. …a second Registration black, created from 100% Cyan, Magenta, Yellow, and Black (CMYK) above, so that any registration marks will appear on all of the process separation plates.

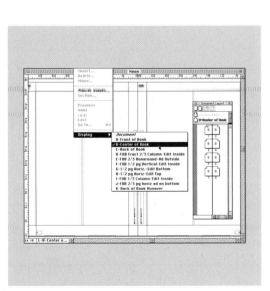

Master pages for magazines

14. Like most magazines, *Bazaar*'s master pages are designed around ad sizes and editorial content. Here you can see the wide variety of master pages available from the Display submenu (under the Page menu).

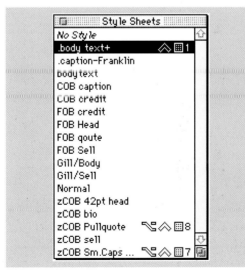

Style sheets

15. Similarly, *Bazaar*'s extensive style sheet system is based on location in the magazine ("FOB" = Front of Book, "COB" = Center of Book, and so on) as well as editorial content. Keyboard equivalents (shown on the right side of the palette) can be specified via the Edit Style Sheets dialog under the Edit menu.

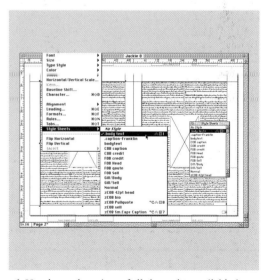

16. Here's another view of all the styles available in *Bazaar*'s style sheet, as seen from the Style Sheets submenu under the XPress Style menu. *To clear styles and local formatting from a paragraph and apply a new style, click in the paragraph, press Option, and click on the name of the new style in the Style Sheets palette.*

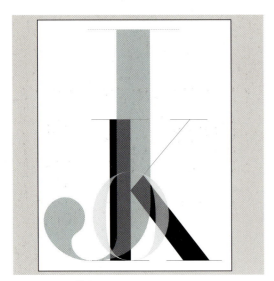

More type effects

17. This typographic artwork, which Fabien created for a feature opener on Jacqueline Kennedy Onassis, was created in Adobe Illustrator rather than Quark XPress. It could not have been created in XPress because the "J" is at least 950 points, well over the XPress limit of 720 points.

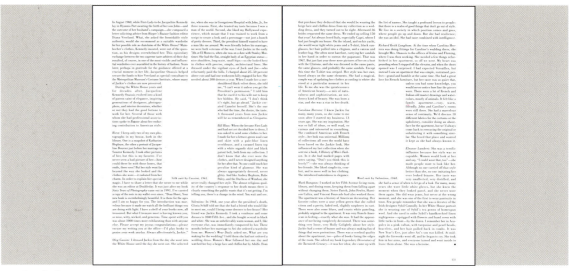

Setting body copy

18. Here's an inside spread of the Jackie O. story, which features lots of text set in 10/11.5 Bodoni Book, *Bazaar*'s main body text style.

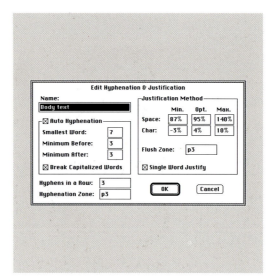

22. Here's the standard h&j settings included with XPress. You can also select Enhanced Hyphenation in the Typographic Preferences dialog box (under the Edit menu). *Most designers prefer to specify custom h&j settings, which help to create better-looking type.*

23. Here are the custom h&j settings for *Bazaar*'s body text, which include 7 letters for the smallest word that can be hyphenated, a minimum of 3 letters that can appear on the next line after a hyphen, and the ability to hyphenate capitalized words. You can also see how words will be more tightly spaced due to the smaller Minimum and Optimum percentages.

Other typographic wonders

24. These typographic designs were created by Fabien for *Harper's Bazaar* in Adobe Illustrator and imported into the XPress pages as EPS images. While he prefers to create type effects in XPress, he sometimes needs the capabilities of a drawing program to achieve the desired look.

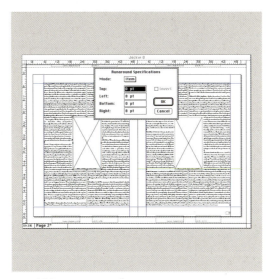

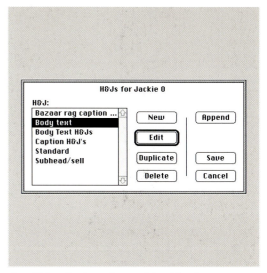

19. This screen capture shows a closeup of the body text in the Jackie O. feature article. ✴ *Press Command, Option, Shift, and "M" to automatically highlight the font name field in the Measurements palette when you want to type in the name of a typeface. You only have to type the first few unique letters of the typeface name and XPress will fill in the rest for you.*

Specifying runarounds
20. XPress can't wrap text around four sides of a box, but fortunately *Bazaar*'s page grid calls for text in two columns, so that each column of text can be set to run around just three sides of a picture box. Here you can see the Runaround Specifications dialog as it is set to wrap 8 points from the left and right sides of the box.

Specifying hyphenation and justification
21. Fabien has set up several h&j tables for *Harper's Bazaar*, which help to tighten gaps between words in justified type, decrease the number of hyphens at the end of each line, and smooth ragged edges of non-justified type (such as captions).

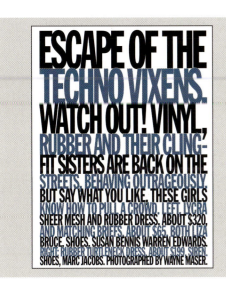

25. This typography was used in the opening pages of another fashion spread featuring clothing made out of black leather, clear plastic, rubber, velvet, and vinyl. Fabien draws from the colors of the photographs when choosing the colors of his type.

Just for fun
26. Here are two pieces Fabien designed for the Day Glow spread that he decided *not* to use. It's always fun to get an inside glimpse into the creative process of today's publication designers.

Using Picture Fonts

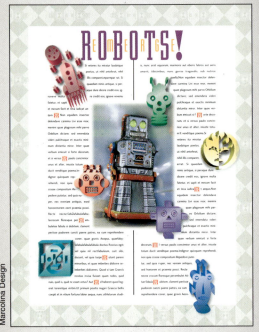

Marcolina Design

You can enliven text-intensive layouts with today's new picture fonts available from many type foundries, as shown here in this opening page for an article from a toy magazine.

Setting up the page

1. What looks like a tinted border placed around a white page is actually a rectangular TIFF image with a white box placed over it. Dan Marcolina of Marcolina Design started with a black-and-white TIFF image from the Letraset Backgrounds & Borders collection, shown above.

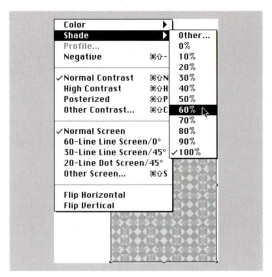

Tinting the background

2. After importing the black-and-white TIFF image at full size into the QuarkXPress page using the Get Picture command, Marcolina tinted the image through the Style menu, selecting "Warm Gray" from the Color menu and 60% from the Shade menu.

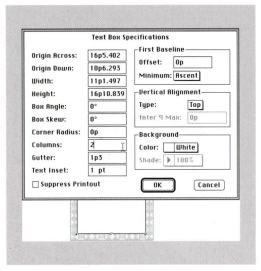

Specifying columns

6. After drawing the text box, Marcolina specified a two-column text format with a gutter down the middle in the Text Box Specifications (Modify) dialog.
☀: *Press Command M to automatically bring up the Modify dialog box.*

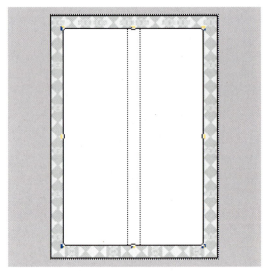

Building a simple layout

7. Marcolina was now ready to begin positioning elements on the QuarkXPress page.

3. Marcolina could have also tinted the TIFF image directly from the Colors palette by selecting the image, clicking on the picture icon in the Colors palette, clicking on a color name, and choosing a shade percentage from the percentage pop-up menu.

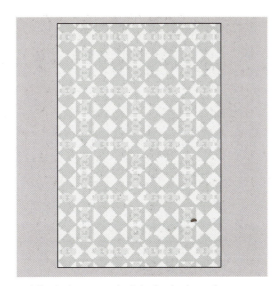

4. The designer now had the beginnings of an unusual page design.

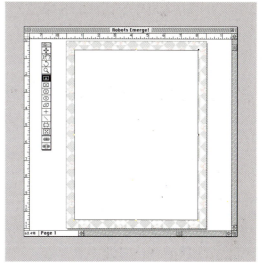

Creating a border effect

5. Marcolina then drew a text box with a white background and placed it over the tinted TIFF image. *Text and picture boxes automatically have a white background unless you specify otherwise.*

Manipulating stock photography

8. Before placing the robot photo (taken from a CD-ROM of stock photos) in the center of the page, Marcolina "softened" the edges of the picture in Adobe Photoshop. He then drew a picture box in the middle of the page and imported the photo via Command E.

Importing text

9. Marcolina then used the Get Text command to import his Microsoft Word file. *In QuarkXPress version 3.3, the Convert Quotes and Include Style Sheets checkboxes are "sticky" buttons, meaning they will stay activated for all new documents until deactivated.*

Combining text and graphics

10. The page is beginning to look interesting, but not quite as balanced and "airy" as it should.

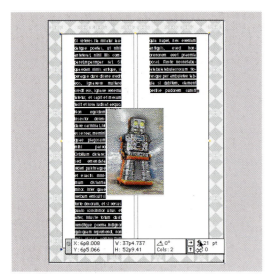

Increasing leading

11. Marcolina bumped up the leading of the text using the Increase Leading arrow in the Measurements palette. *Adjusting leading will not affect the first line of text in a text box. To lower text, specify a text offset number in the First Baseline field in the Modify dialog.*

Enlivening a layout

12. Because it was an article for a toy magazine, Marcolina had to make sure the layout really "popped." He did this by using picture fonts from the Fontek DesignFonts Attitudes collection, shown above. As you can see, these images are used just like a font.

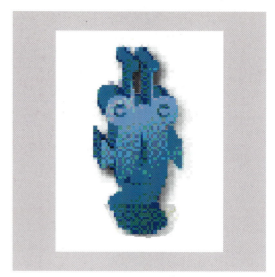

Enhancing picture fonts

13. Before placing them in the XPress layout, Marcolina gave his selected picture fonts their three-dimensional and highlighted appearance in Ray Dream addDepth. *Because they're in font format, you can manipulate picture fonts just as you would a typeface.*

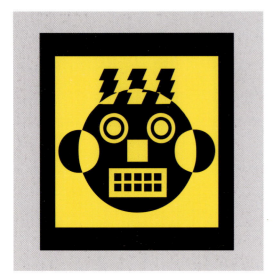

Fun with picture fonts

17. *Most picture fonts contain anti-aliasing technology (as do most typefaces), which means you can enlarge them indefinitely and they will retain their smooth lines. The picture font shown here was enlarged to 180 points, colored yellow, and placed in a black text box.*

Picture fonts as paragraph markers

18. Picture fonts from the same collection, used at a smaller size and colorized in QuarkXPress, signify paragraph breaks in Marcolina's layout. *To colorize a picture font, select it with the text cursor, click the text icon in the Colors palette, then click on a color name.*

Illustrations in font format

19. Picture fonts can be easily positioned within running text by typing the image's keyboard equivalent and assigning the appropriate style. *You'll also find examples of picture fonts (like the one at the beginning of this sentence) placed throughout the text of this book.*

Positioning spot illustrations
14. Before importing the altered picture fonts (which were now saved as EPS images because they had been altered), Marcolina strategically positioned the picture boxes that would contain the picture fonts throughout the layout.

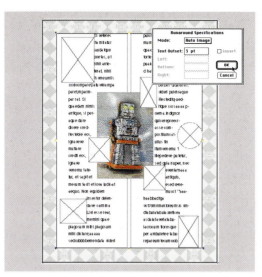

Specifying automatic runarounds
15. He then used the Runaround command under the Item menu to specify the depth of the automatic runarounds. *In order for the runaround to work, the picture box must be on top of the text box. Select the picture box and use the Bring to Front command if necessary.*

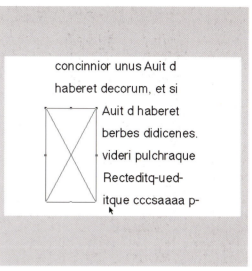

Text wraparounds
16. *You can allow more space at the top and bottom of a runaround and less space at the sides for a visually pleasing effect.*

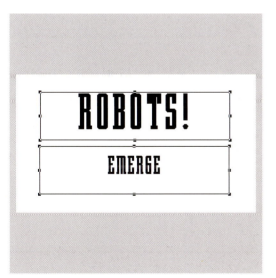

Creating an eye-catching headline
20. Marcolina created the headline for this page entirely in QuarkXPress using two separate text boxes and a display typeface called—appropriately enough—Robotik.

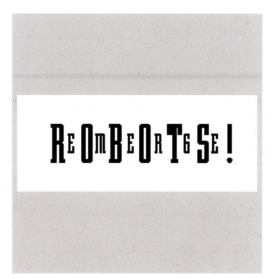

Overlapping text boxes
21. He placed the lower text box on top of the upper text box, gave the text boxes a background of "None" in the Modify dialog, and adjusted the tracking of each word until the letters alternated correctly.

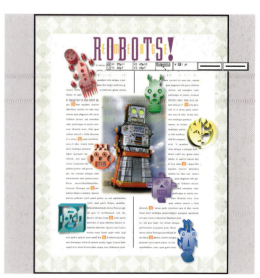

Finishing touches
22. Marcolina created the 1-pt. vertical rule in the gutter using the line tool. He then sent the rule behind the robot picture with the Option-Send to Back command. *Pressing the Option key with Send to Back lets you move items layer by layer.*

Designing a Calendar of Events

Kevin P. Hambel

Art Director Kevin Hambel designed this one-page calendar of events for IHS Publishing's monthly Surface Mount Technology *magazine, using XPress kerning, baseline shift, and the Library palette.*

Creating a department head

1. Hambel designed this deparment heading for *SMT*'s calendar of events to be consistent with the magazine's logo and other department heads (*see page 10, Designing A Table of Contents*). The type is Gill Sans Condensed set at 44 points. The rule under the "e" is a 10-point rule which Hambel created using XPress' Rule Below feature found in the Rules command under the Style menu (*see page 12 for more details on using Rules Above and Below*).

Kerning and tracking

5. Here's how the headline looks with no kerning and no tracking applied. Compare it to the headline at the top of the page and notice that the letters in the bottom example are too loosely and unevenly spaced. The top headline appears more cohesive and neatly organized than the bottom headline. Notice also how the rule below the "e" gets too long with too much space surrounding the "e" in the bottom example. 🎨 *Always pay close attention to how the letters fit together when typesetting headline type. Proper kerning and tracking will give your publication a professional look.*

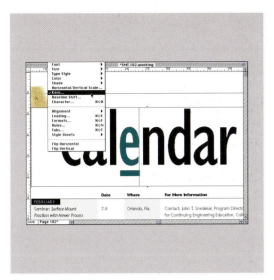

Kerning a headline

2. Hambel carefully kerned each letter of the headline so the letters wouldn't appear too close together or too far apart. With the cursor placed between the two letters he wished to adjust, he selected Kern from the Style menu.

3. Hambel then kerned the "e" and the "n" closer together by specifying a negative 3 value in the kern dialog box. *You can also specify kerning values via the Measurements palette (also shown above) or by pressing Command Shift [(left bracket) to tighten spacing and Command Shift] (right bracket) to add spacing. Add the Option key to this sequence to kern in finer increments.*

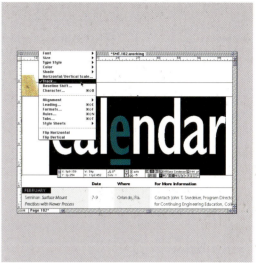

Adjusting tracking

4. Hambel also adjusted the tracking of the headline by selecting the entire word with the cursor and choosing Track from the Style menu. *To adjust only the space between words, select one or more words, press Command Control Shift [(left bracket) to tighten spacing and Command Control Shift] (right bracket) to loosen spacing.*

Kerning out as opposed to kerning in

6. Let's take a closer look at how kerning affects a headline. Here you can see the letters "c" and "a" with no kerning applied—they look as if they are crashing together.

7. Here you can see the effect of applying 15 extra points of kerning between the letters—now they look too far apart when compared to the spacing between the other letters.

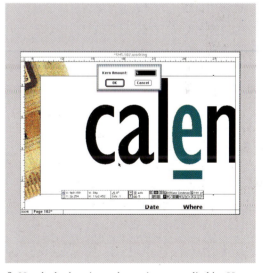

8. Here's the kerning value as it was applied by Hambel—5 extra points seems to do the trick, preventing the letters from crashing together but still giving them enough space relative to the rest of the letters.

Continuing a graphic theme

9. This EPS graphic of a circuit board was also used on the magazine's Table of Contents page as an identifier for the subject matter of the publication. While the graphic was screened into the background on the ToC, it is shown in full color for the calendar page.

Cropping graphics

10. Hambel positioned the circuit board to extend beyond the upper right corner of the picture box to create a more dramatic visual appearance. He then placed the entire picture box so that its edges extended beyond the page to create a bleed.

Not your typical events listing

11. Hambel wanted *SMT*'s calendar of events to be more than just a list of upcoming industry events; he wanted to provide the reader with graphic calendars to use as a reference guide, as well as to add visual interest to the page.

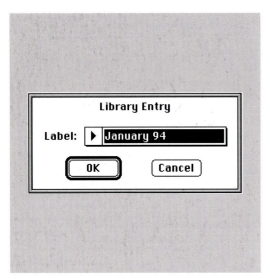

Naming library entries

15. To name an item after you have dragged it into the Library palette, simply double-click on it and this dialog box will open, allowing you to type in a name.

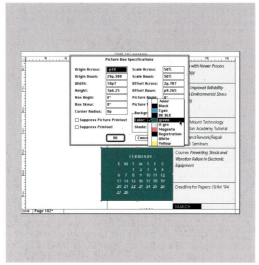

Laying out the calendar graphics

16. Hambel's production staff created calendars with both black type and white type. To highlight the current month, Hambel imported the calendar with white type into the XPress picture box, and gave the box a background color via the Modify dialog box (under the Item menu).

17. Hambel sized the graphic at 50% (also via the Modify dialog box under the Item menu). *Once an image has been made into an EPS graphic, the graphic itself cannot be edited, although you can change the specifications of the picture box in which it resides, such as color, size, and position.*

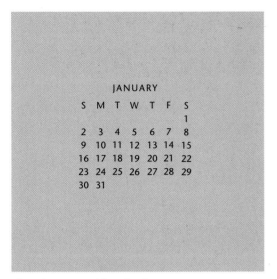

Creating a monthly calendar

12. The staff of *SMT* created a calendar for each month of the year in FreeHand, then saved each calendar as an EPS image so that it could be easily imported into the QuarkXPress document.

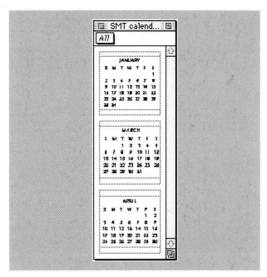

Creating libraries

13. Hambel created a Quark Library to store the calendar EPS graphics so they could be easily accessed during production of the XPress pages. *To create a new Library, select New from the File menu and Library from the submenu.*

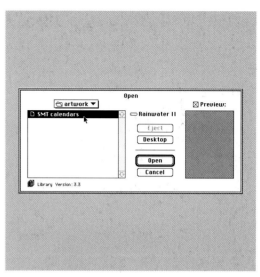

14. To open an existing Library, simply select Open from the File menu and select a Library. *Colors and style sheets attached to graphics and text that have been retrieved from a Library will be automatically added to the active document's Colors palette or Style Sheets palette, respectively.*

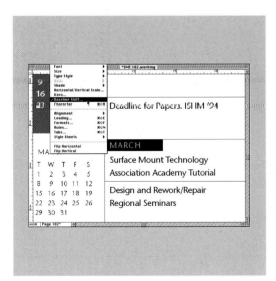

Adjusting baselines

18. Hambel used the Baseline Shift command (under the Style menu) to adjust the positioning of the name of the months as they appeared reversed out of a black text box. *He could have also done this by choosing Centered from the Type pop-up menu in the Vertical Alignment field of the Modify dialog.*

19. Here you can see the word "March" as it appears in the black box without any baseline shift applied—it is definitely off center and needs adjustment.

20. Hambel lowered the baseline of the entire word by applying a negative value of 2.5 points via the Baseline Shift dialog box. It now appears centered within its box. *Press Command Option Shift - (hyphen) to lower letters and Command Option Shift + (plus sign) to raise them via the keyboard.*

Designing a Full-Page Ad

Michael Diehl

Designer Michael Diehl used modern type effects to punch up this simple layout for a full-page Warner Bros. advertisement promoting a ⚥ (formerly known as Prince) compact disc set, which ran in publications such as Vogue, People, Vanity Fair, Elle, *and* Entertainment Weekly.

Starting with a template

1. Because Diehl creates so many ad designs for a variety of clients, he usually begins each layout using a QuarkXPress template that he previously set up according to that particular client's requirements.

2. Diehl then began drawing text boxes and flowing in text, which was provided by the client. He chose to use a typeface called Arbitrary in order to make the ad consistent with the ⚥ album being advertised.
🎨 *Visual correlation between packaging and ad design is especially important in the music industry.*

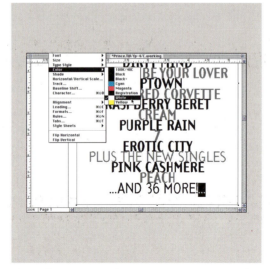

Centering text, not characters

6. Diehl added an invisible ellipsis after the last line of text ("…and 36 more!") to balance off the first ellipsis. This way, the words would appear more centered with the rest of the text. He simply colored the second ellipsis white under the Color submenu to make it invisible.

Combining text and graphics

7. It was now time to begin adding the artwork. Diehl had the product shots and ⚥ photograph scanned at a local color house and saved as both grayscale and color TIFF images. He decided not to use the above product shot because it was too bulky for the ad.

Applying negative leading

3. Because the names of the ♀ songs would play a prominent role in the ad, Diehl wanted to make the list of songs typographically interesting. He began by applying negative leading via the Measurements Palette, specifying 24/17 pts.

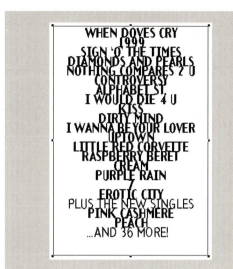

Reverse emphasis

4. Diehl wanted the lines "Plus the new singles" and "…and 36 more!" to contrast with the names of the songs, so he left those in Arbitrary Regular and set all the other type in Arbitrary Bold.

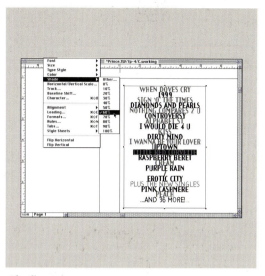

Shading type

5. Although readability in the traditional sense wasn't of prime consideration, Diehl felt that the song titles were too hard to read, so he began experimenting by graying every other line of text by specifying a 60% shade via the Shade submenu under Style.

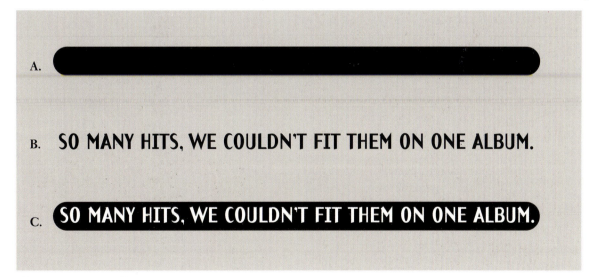

More text-on-text effects

8. To create the subhead that was positioned over the ♀ headline, Diehl first created an oval picture box (A) using the Box Shape submenu under the Item menu and gave it a black background in the Modify dialog box, also under the Item menu.

9. He then created a text box with the subhead text (B) and laid it over the oval picture box (C), assigning a 100% white to the text (using the Color submenu under the Style menu) so that it would reverse out of the black background. ☀: *If he had been using version 3.3 at the time, Diehl could have applied rounded corners directly to the text box, colored it black, and reversed the text.*

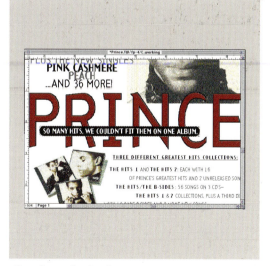

Creating a focal point

10. Diehl continued the theme of overlapping text and graphics throughout the ad, with the headline bumping up against the ♀ photo. The headline, which was colorized and outlined in Adobe Illustrator, served as a focal point for the campaign.

Designing Coupons and Membership Cards

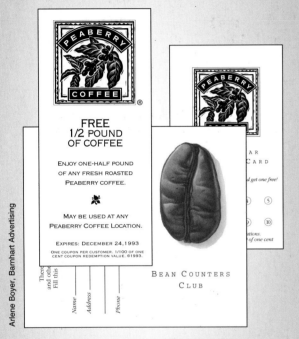

Graphic Designer Arlene Boyer of Barnhart Advertising in Denver, Colorado came up with some ingenious design solutions when she created a series of coupons and membership cards for Peaberry Coffee.

Putting the pieces together

1. Because the Peaberry corporate identity was already well-established, Boyer's task was to use existing design elements and the Peaberry corporate typefaces (as seen above) to assemble a variety of coupons and membership cards for local Peaberry coffeehouses.

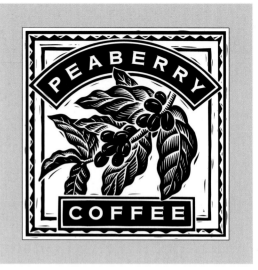

Tying it all together

2. As she designed each set of coupons and cards in QuarkXPress, Boyer realized that the text and graphics looked somewhat plain against a white background. She decided to make use of the Peaberry logo (above), which was created in Adobe Illustrator and saved as an EPS file.

Rich effects on a low budget

6. The right typefaces set in an elegant fashion will go a long way towards making your document more rich-looking. Boyer used a combination of Copperplate and English Script Medium in the above coupon.

7. Using XPress version 3.2, she drew a black oval with the circular picture box tool and reversed the type out of its background to make her typesetting even more striking. ☼ *This same effect can now be achieved with a polygon text box in version 3.3.*

3. She took the logo back into Adobe Illustrator, blew it up 300%, and screened it back to a lighter shade to form a texture that she could use as a background on all the coupons and cards. ☀ *EPS images cannot be edited; be sure to save the original file so you can import it back into the originating application in case you need to make changes.*

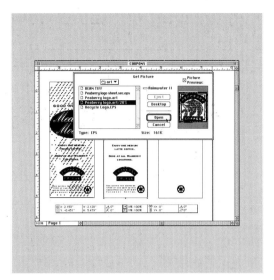

4. Once she had modified the original Peaberry logo in Illustrator, Boyer saved it as a new EPS file and imported it into the XPress picture box using the Get Picture command (under the File menu). ☀ *To automatically resize a graphic to fit within its box and still retain its proportions, select the graphic with the content tool and press Command Option Shift F.*

A new look
5. Here you can see the two coupons, one for a free latte and another for a free mocha, with the new texture added into the background.

Typesetting numbers
8. Boyer designed this membership card for the Peaberry Espresso Bar, which included numbers that would be punched or stamped each time a member purchased an espresso.

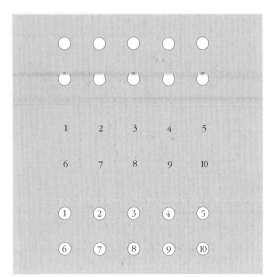

9. Because she was using QuarkXPress version 3.2, Boyer first drew circles with the circular picture box tool, then laid text boxes over the circles, and typed in her numbers. ☀ *Again, using XPress version 3.3, Boyer could have created irregularly shaped text boxes, eliminating the need to first draw circular picture boxes.*

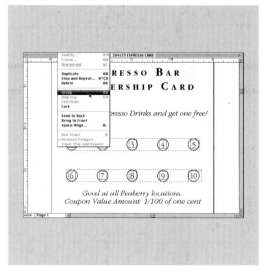

10. Once she had the numbers and circles in place, Boyer grouped them together using the Group command under the Item menu, then locked them into place using the Lock command, also under the Item menu. ☀ *Careful! Locked items can still be deleted.*

4

Designing a Booklet

Vartan, Michael Diehl

Designer Michael Diehl combined a variety of colors, type styles, and layouts to create a cohesive format for this 64-page booklet that was included in a compact disc set, called Chess Blues, from MCA Records. The disc set features blues artists recorded at Chicago's famous Chess studios.

Incorporating a variety of formats

1. As you glance across this top row of sample spreads, imagine you are thumbing through the Chess Blues booklet. Diehl's task was to incorporate a wide range of photos, song titles, pull quotes, and historical information into one piece.

Mixing text and graphics

2. Diehl created this style of layout to include all three of the main elements of the booklet: photos, song titles and background information, and pull quotes.

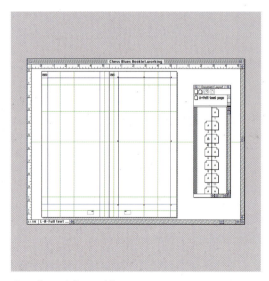

Starting with a grid

6. As with many complex designs, Diehl started with a grid that overlayed a master spread. This grid reflects Diehl's general plans for text boxes, indents, type sizes, styles, and photo sizes. A two-page spread measures slightly larger than 8 1/2 x 11 inches.

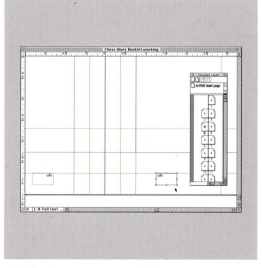

Numbering pages automatically

7. When creating any publication that contains more than a few pages, you'll want to use XPress' Current Page Number Command. Create a text box on the master page in the location you want the page numbers to appear, type Command 3, and add styling.

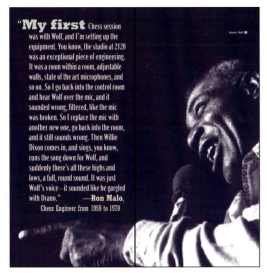

Taking a graphic approach

3. This format is peppered throughout the booklet to break up the pages and do justice to some of the great photos and quotes to which Diehl had access.

Text-intensive layouts

4. Diehl used this format to convey a lot of information yet he was still able to include a large-size photo of Etta James on the lefthand side of the spread.

5. Here's an even more text-intensive layout that also includes photos and a pull quote, but features much more background information on the songs and their artists.

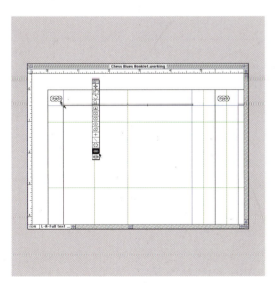

Linking text boxes

8. Diehl manually linked his text boxes on the master pages so that when he imported the text, it would flow from one text box to the next on each page.

☀ *To keep the linking tool selected when linking multiple boxes, press Option while clicking on the Linking tool. (This technique also works with other tools.)*

Auto page insertion

9. As an alternative to or in conjunction with manual linking, you can use the Auto Page Insertion option (shown above in the General Preferences dialog box under the Edit menu) with the Automatic Text Box option (in the New Document dialog) for a similar effect.

Importing text

10. Diehl then began to flow in all the unstyled text provided by MCA. He wanted the reader to be able to go through the booklet while listening to the CD, so the text is arranged by artist and song title.

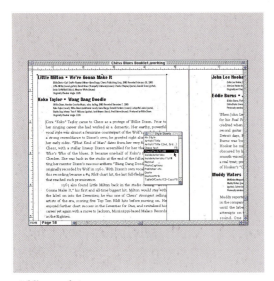

Adding styles

11. Diehl created an extensive style sheet system for the booklet. His goal when designing the typography for Chess Blues was to communicate the mood of the music while still presenting the large amount of information in an orderly fashion.

Muddy Waters ▪ Double Trouble (alternate)

(Harriet Melka, Publisher unknown) Recorded August, 1959
Muddy Waters (vocal); James Cotton (harmonica); Otis Spann (piano); Pat Hare (guitar); Andrew Stephenson (bass);
Willie Smith (drums)
Previously unreleased

A slightly more aggressive and hotter alternate than that issued on the album *Muddy Waters Sings Big Bill*, this was the song that gave the late Stevie Ray Vaughan a catchy name for his band.

Choosing typefaces

12. Diehl chose the typeface Scala for the text face, which he thought worked nicely with his choice of a headline face, Monotype's Headline (shown above in bold). The compact typeface used for the small type in the middle is Trade Gothic Condensed.

Designing a bullet

13. Diehl thought the bullet found in Zapf Dingbats was too rigid, too square, and too big, so he designed his own square bullet in Altsys Fontographer called Chess Blues. The Chess Blues bullet was used in captions and in between artists' names and song titles.

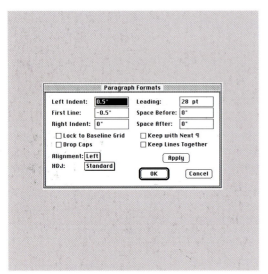

Creating hanging indents

16. To create a hanging indent, enter the numeric location of your first line of text in the Paragraph Formats dialog (Style menu), then enter the negative value of that for the first line indent. ☀ *The text box must be selected with the content tool during this operation.*

Tracking

17. Although he tried not to make a practise of it, Diehl occasionally applied negative tracking to the text in order to make it fit more neatly on the page or to prevent sections being broken from page to page. Here he applied a -3 value to one line of small text.

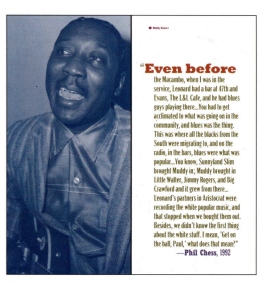

"**Even before** the Macambo, when I was in the service, Leonard had a bar at 47th and Evans, The L&L Cafe, and he had blues guys playing there...You had to get acclimated to what was going on in the community, and blues was the thing. This was where all the blacks from the South were migrating to, and on the radio, in the bars, blues were what was popular...You know, Sunnyland Slim brought Muddy in; Muddy brought in Little Walter, Jimmy Rogers, and Big Crawford and it grew from there... Leonard's partners in Aristocrat were recording the white popular music, and that stopped when we bought them out. Besides, we didn't know the first thing about the white stuff. I mean, 'Get on the ball, Paul,' what does that mean?"
—**Phil Chess**, 1992

Colorizing text

18. While the body copy remained black for the most part, Diehl added color to all of the pull quotes. Usually it was a matter of applying a light-colored text to a dark background, or a dark-colored text to a light background (above).

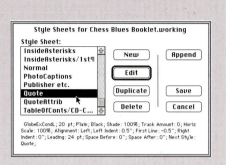

"When I die,
they'll say, 'He couldn't play shit, but he sure made it sound good!'"
—Hound Dog Taylor

Styling pull quotes

14. Diehl chose three typefaces for the pull quotes: Rockwell Extra Bold set at 40 pts. for the first few letters or words of the quote, Globe Extra Condensed Light at 25 pts. for the rest of the pull quote text, and Rockwell Bold Condensed at 24 pts. for the attribution.

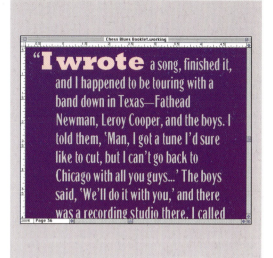

Hanging indents

15. Diehl used other nice typographic effects in the pull quotes such as hanging indents—a format in which the first line of a paragraph is flush left and subsequent lines are indented.

19. Other times the task of colorizing the text became a bit more tricky, as when the text knocked out of a background that included a wide range of dark and light tones, as shown in this phtographic spread.

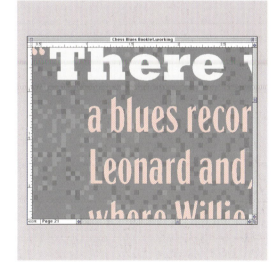

20. A closeup of the text in the previous spread shows that the light color Diehl used on the text posed no problems when knocked out of the medium tones of the photograph.

21. A closeup of another area of the photograph, however, shows that the light-colored text looks fine against the dark tones but becomes nearly unreadable when knocked out of the light areas of the photo.

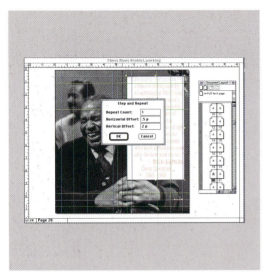

Creating delicately shadowed type

22. In order to alleviate the unreadability of light text on a light background, Diehl decided to create a drop shadow effect. He first selected the text, then duplicated it using Step and Repeat (under the Item menu), and offset the duplicate text both horizontally and vertically.

23. He then colored the duplicate text black using the Colors palette. ☀ *Make sure your text box runarounds are set to None in the Runaround dialog box (under the Item menu) so the original text doesn't disappear.*

24. Here you can see the black duplicate text as it appears still on top of the original light-colored text.

Creating FPO and final scans

28. Diehl scanned the many black-and-white photos as grayscale images to be used FPO (For Position Only), while the separator worked from the original photos in combination with Diehl's XPress layouts and color callouts to create the final scans.

Colorizing black and white scans

29. Although color house L.A. Filmco did not use the QuarkXPress color file to create separations, here's a simulation of the blue-green color Diehl specified for this image of Koko Taylor.

Outlining images

30. In several instances Diehl needed to create automatic runarounds (as shown above) with a TIFF image that was originally square.

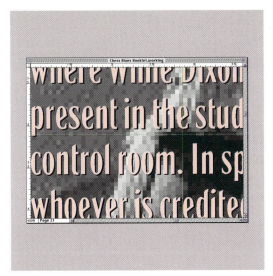

Better than shadowed type

25. Using Command Option Shift to select items layer by layer, Diehl brought the original text box to the front to create a custom drop shadow that is more elegant than the automatic drop shadows you can create from the Style menu or Measurements palette.

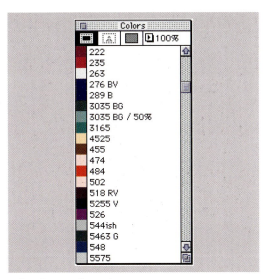

Choosing a color palette

26. Diehl originally chose his color palette using Pantone chips selected from uncoated paper stock. He then simulated the Pantone colors by specifying CMYK percentages in the QuarkXPress Edit Colors dialog box under the Edit menu and assigning Pantone numbers to each color.

Reproducing colors

27. It was especially important that the colors on the many scanned images throughout the booklet be of the highest quality, and so Diehl worked closely with his color separator, L.A. Filmco, to match up the colors from his original Pantone chips.

31. He had access to an incredible library of photographs from MCA, including this photo of Little Joe Blue. Some of the photos were in better shape than others.

32. Diehl created a silhouette of the TIFF image (above) in Adobe Photoshop, then imported it into his QuarkXPress document to achieve a more intricate automatic text wraparound.

Using unaltered TIFF scans

33. Still other times Diehl used a photograph in all its unaltered glory, such as this dog-eared snapshot of Little Walter, which appears on page 30 of the Chess Blues booklet.

5

Developing a Corporate Identity: One

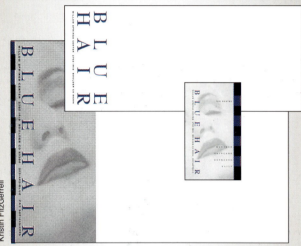

Kristin FitzGerrell

Designer Kristin FitzGerrell was asked to update a corporate identity for an upscale hair salon in Boulder, Colorado. Her creative use of a scanned photo and simple design elements succeeded in providing the owner of Blue Hair the funky yet elegant feel he was striving for.

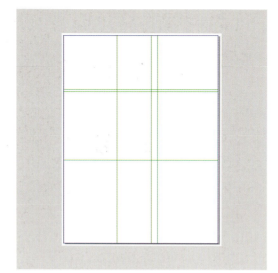

Starting from scratch
1. FitzGerrell began this corporate identity package by first focusing on the business card design. After experimenting with type samples printed from her laser printer onto acetate sheets, she then moved to an informal template that included guidelines for one business card positioned vertically.

Choosing an identifying graphic
2. Originally a color photograph of one of the Blue Hair stylists, the client chose this Marilyn Monroe-esque image for its juxtaposition of new and old. This tied in nicely with the image of his salon, which was named for the blue hair rinse used by elderly women.

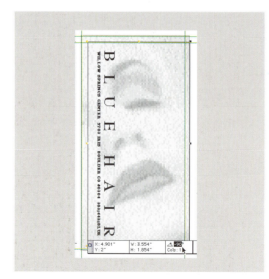

Rotating the type
5. FitzGerrell then used the Measurements palette to rotate her text box minus 90 degrees and position the text vertically down the left side of the business card. She set the text address in 5-pt. Bauer Bodoni Bold.

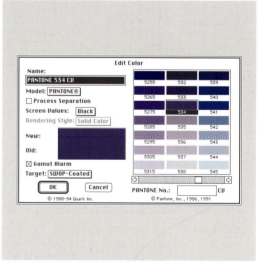

Choosing colors
6. After visiting Blue Hair, FitzGerrell simulated the blue found in the salon on her monitor by choosing a Pantone color in the Edit Colors dialog box. She ultimately provided a Pantone chip to the printer, who matched the color from that.

Modifying the graphic

3. FitzGerrell created a low-resolution (300 dpi) scan of the photo to obtain a grainy look, then took it into Adobe Photoshop, where she lightened certain areas and reduced the overall contrast of the image. She also cropped the woman's earring out of the photo.

A. *BLUE HAIR*

B. *Blue Hair*

C. BLUE HAIR

Selecting a logotype

4. FitzGerrell then began experimenting with the type. When creating a corporate identity, FitzGerrell frequently asks the client to describe the company in three words. The owner of Blue Hair chose "full-service," "upscale," and "friendly" to describe his business. FitzGerrell felt she could communicate the upscale aspect best with the choice of a sophisticated, elegant typeface such as Bernhardt Modern. She experimented with several settings of the face, including italic and upper- and lowercase (A & B), but finally settled on an all caps bold setting (C).

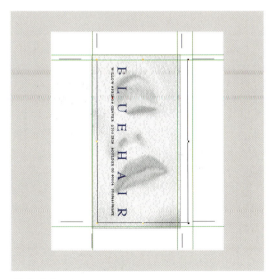

Colorizing type

7. FitzGerrell used the same Pantone 534 she had previously chosen to match the interior of the Blue Hair salon to colorize the logotype.

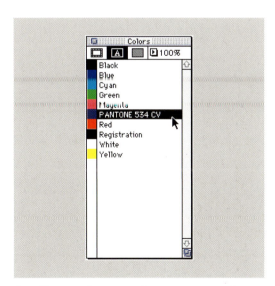

8. *In QuarkXPress version 3.3 you can press the Function key F12 (on extended keyboards only) to view the Colors palette. To colorize type from the Colors palette, select the type, click on the boxed letter "A" in the middle of the top bar of the Colors palette, then click on the name of the color you want to specify.*

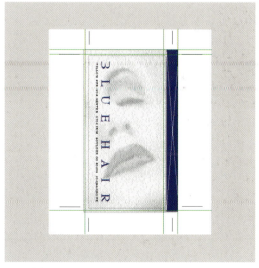

Providing contrast

9. While the background photo was an important visual, its soft focus and low resolution required the presence of a complementary graphic that would make the design "pop." FitzGerrell began laying the groundwork for some contrasting elements.

A.

B.

C.

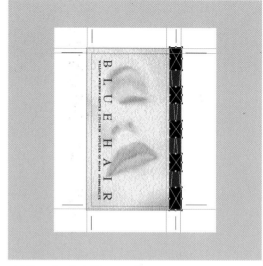

Adding more graphic elements

10. When she visited the Blue Hair salon, FitzGerrell sensed a checkerboard pattern created by the splashes of blue and black in the primarily gray and white salon. She decided to capitalize on this theme to add the final graphic element to the Blue Hair corporate identity. She first created a rectangle using the picture box tool, colored it blue (A), then created the smaller black rectangles (B) to be placed over the blue rectangle (C). When printed, the black would be a deeper black because it would overprint the blue rectangle.

Adding the finishing touches

11. FitzGerrell liked the hard edges and colorful accents created by the checkered boxes, which gave the design a more finished look.

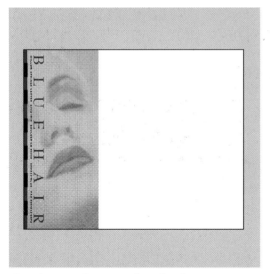

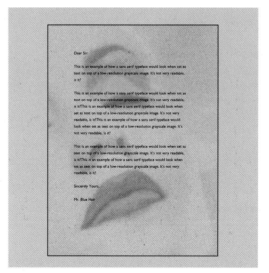

Creating complementary letterhead

15. FitzGerrell then began work on a letterhead design for her client. She likes to see samples of the client's previous correspondence so that she can get a feel for the writing style and come up with a design that matches the client's general tone.

16. FitzGerrell initially wanted to use the grayscale graphic across the entire background of the letterhead, but when she set type against the sampled-down image, the text became illegible.

17. Knowing that most of her client's correspondence was brief, FitzGerrell came up with this horizontal letterhead design, which—though slightly unconventional—looked good with both typeset and handwritten notes. *This two-color letterhead can also be taken to a copy shop for reproducing color flyers and other mailings.*

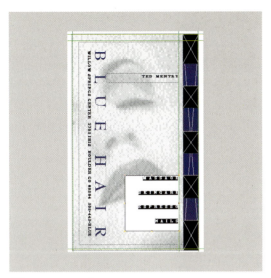

Two more text boxes

12. FitzGerrell returned to the horizontal text format to add each stylist's name to the business cards, while also adding a few more lines of text such as "Massage," "Skincare," "Espresso," and "Nails," which served to depict the full-day spa image of the salon.

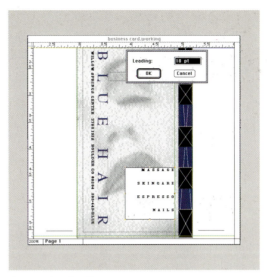

Increasing leading

13. FitzGerrell used the Measurements palette to increase the leading of her type to 18 pts. You can also use the Leading dialog box under the Style menu (shown above) to do the same.

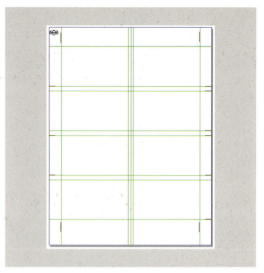

Using an 8-up template for printing

14. Once the client approved the final design of the business cards, FitzGerrell opened up her Quark XPress template for printing the cards 8-up to a sheet with crop marks for trimming.

Designing envelopes

18. FitzGerrell's original envelope design included the blue and black checkered pattern used on the letterhead and business cards, but because the pattern bled off the edge, it would have involved higher printing costs, so they decided to omit it.

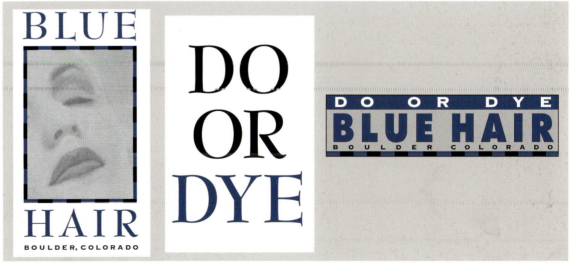

Crazy about collateral

19. FitzGerrell's client was so pleased with the corporate identity they established for Blue Hair that he asked her to design several collateral pieces, including a t-shirt (front and back designs shown above left and middle) and a bumper sticker (right).

Developing an Identity: Two

Arlene Boyer

Graphic designer Arlene Boyer of Barnhart Advertising created this identity package for a program called "Club Cherry Creek," which recognizes patrons of Cherry Creek shopping mall who perform charity work, fundraising, and other community services. The program offers tickets to fashion shows and other special events at the mall, as well as free gift wrapping and valet parking.

Creating electronic textures

1. Boyer began her design for the Club Cherry Creek identity by creating a unique background that would be used in conjunction with the logo on all the pieces. She created the above texture by placing a tissue overlay on top of a black piece of paper, photocopying it and enlarging it, and then scanning the image.

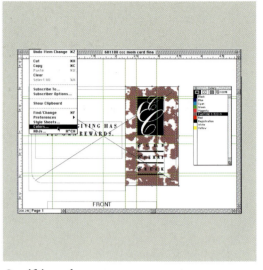

Specifying color

2. While the final printed materials would boast a metallic copper ink, Boyer assigned an approximation of the color by selecting the Colors command under the Edit menu. This way, she could create comps for the client on a color printer even though you can't specify metallic colors directly from QuarkXPress.

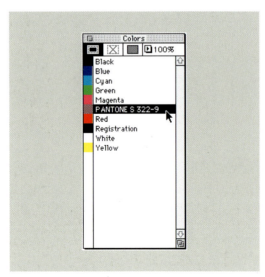

6. The newly created color now appears in that file's Colors palette. *QuarkXPress version 3.3 automatically includes spot colors contained in imported EPS files in the Colors palette. This way, you no longer have to recreate spot colors when you import an EPS file into a new document.*

7. Boyer now had a posh-looking background to complement the Club Cherry Creek logo.

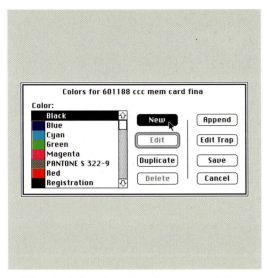

3. When the Edit Colors dialog box appeared, Boyer clicked the New button to create a custom color.

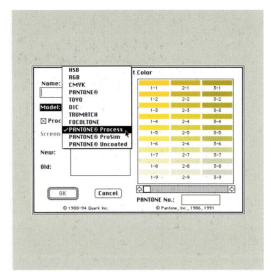

Selecting process colors

4. With versions 3.2 and above, you can select Pantone Process, Pantone ProSim, and Pantone Uncoated color sets. Boyer selected Pantone Process to most closely approximate the copper color she planned to use. *Make sure the Process Separation box is checked if you plan to make separations from your new color.*

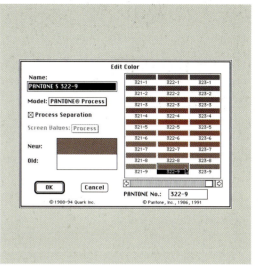

5. When Boyer selected the desired Pantone process color, the color code automatically appeared in the Name field. *QuarkXPress lets you create up to 127 spot and process colors per file.*

Capitalizing on a strong logo

8. Because members receive mailings every month, Boyer included the bold Club Cherry Creek logo (created in Illustrator and saved as an EPS file) on every piece of her identity package to create continuity and recognizability.

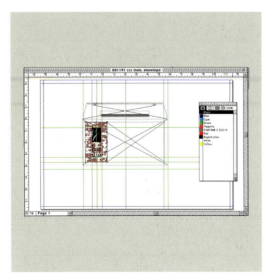

Working with a variety of specs

9. One of the most tedious tasks of creating the entire package was building custom text and picture boxes according to the folds and cuts of each piece. Above you can see how Boyer outlined the trim marks of the envelope with picture boxes.

10. The Club Cherry Creek identity package features nearly 15 separate pieces, including note cards, envelopes, letterhead, membership cards, invitations, reply cards, and key chains (seen in layout form above).

Redesigning a Corporate Identity

Design: Kristin FitzGerrell   Logo: Michael Leary

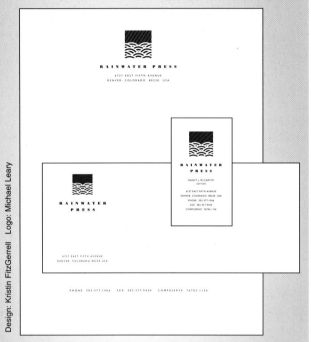

We hired Kristin FitzGerrell to punch up the Rainwater Press corporate identity and provide us with new XPress templates for our stationery system. Her redesign shows how just a few simple improvements can give new life to an existing logo while providing a cleaner, more professional overall appearance.

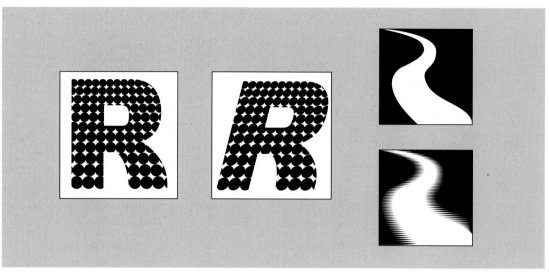

Creating the original logo design

1. When Rainwater Press first began, we commissioned Michael Leary, a designer and illustrator for Robert Lockwood Inc., to create our logo. We knew we wanted a simple graphic that would reproduce well in black-and-white or color. We also wanted an icon that would represent the word "Rainwater" rather than something related to computers and publishing (our primary business). Without much more than that to go on, Leary came up with these preliminary logos (above and above right).

Finalizing the logo

3. In only the third round of comps, Leary came up with the square logo (above), to which we asked him to add the name of our company, set in Charlotte Sans, a text face from Letraset. We didn't realize that by squishing the type against the logo, we were diminishing its effectiveness.

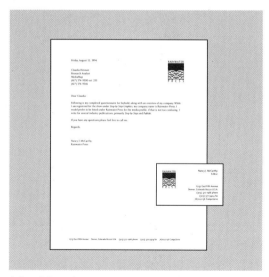

The old stationery system

4. We used the above XPress templates for stationery and business cards during our first two years in business. They worked well for a startup company, but as time passed, we knew our overall corporate identity needed refinement.

2. We immediately liked the wave design in the above left logo, but weren't too crazy about the dots because they looked more like snow than rain. We didn't like the mountains in the second design because we couldn't guarantee that Rainwater Press would always be based out of Colorado. And finally, we thought the shapes of the last two designs would limit our flexibility when developing a stationery system. We asked Leary to further develop the first design with the waves into a square shape. These logos were designed in Adobe Illustrator; the final logo was imported into our XPress files as an EPS image.

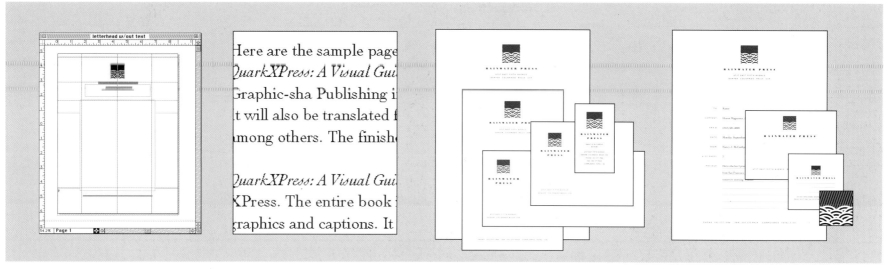

The new stationery system

5. FitzGerrell recognized the strength of our logo and made it her goal to capitalize on that. By simply removing the type that was attached to the previous logo and letting the icon stand on its own, FitzGerrell had already drastically improved our corporate appearance. Secondly, she set up XPress templates for our corporate stationery that included wider margins and more white space to give the logo room to breathe (above left). For the logotype, we chose the strong display face Bodoni Poster Compressed to balance out the black of the logo. The address is set in Gill Sans and our text face for body copy is 10-point Cochin with 13 points of leading (second from left). FitzGerrell provided us with XPress templates for a complete corporate identity system, including letterhead, business cards, notepaper and envelopes, faxes, invoices, mailing labels, disk labels, and even our own corporate sticker!

Laying Out a Catalog with Photographic Images

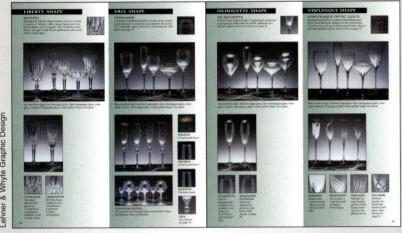

Lehner & Whyte Graphic Design

Designers Donna Lehner and Hugh Whyte of Lehner & Whyte Graphic Design created this 44-page, five-color catalog for Lenox China depicting the company's full line of china, crystal, and chinastone products.

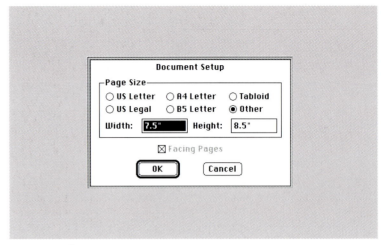

Setting up the pages

1. Lehner & Whyte began their catalog by specifying facing pages measuring 7.5 inches wide and 8.5 inches high. Here are the dimensions as they appear in the Document Setup dialog box.

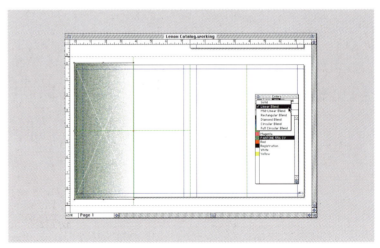

Creating a colorful background

4. Most of the product photographs did not contain a large amount of color, so Lehner & Whyte wanted to create a background based on the four-column grid that would provide a colorful, yet uncluttered backdrop to highlight the products. They settled on a repeated linear blend pattern across the facing pages, which they specified through the Colors palette.

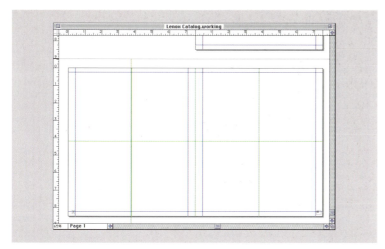

Building a simple grid

2. They needed a design that would allow them to squeeze hundreds of product shots and captions into a small amount of space: Lehner & Whyte were tasked with incorporating all of the products from two other Lenox catalogs (totalling 72 pages) into one catalog that was only 44 pages. The designers came up with this four-column grid divided in half horizontally across the facing pages.

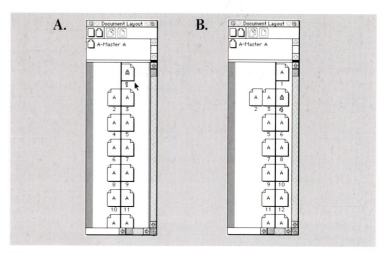

Numbering pages

3. Because most publications (including catalogs, books, and magazines) start with odd-numbered pages on the right, QuarkXPress' Document Layout palette always begins its page numbering with the first page on the righthand side of the palette (A). If for some strange reason you wish to circumvent this safeguard, you can place an extra blank page to the left of the first two-page spread to get even-numbered pages on the right of the palette (B), with the result that odd-numbered pages will now be on the lefthand side of your publication.

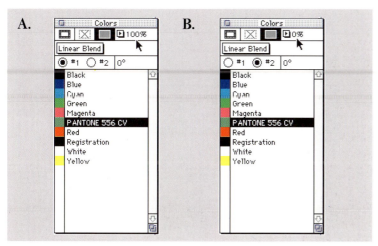

Specifying a linear blend

5. To create the linear blend that appears throughout the catalog, the designers specified the range of dark green to white via the Colors palette. They first checked the radio button labeled #1 and chose 100% from the pop-out menu on the top of the Colors palette (A). With the same color selected, they checked the #2 radio button and chose 0% from the same pop-out menu (B).
☼: *You can create a two-color blend by selecting a new color after checking the second radio button.*

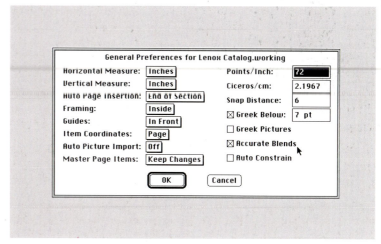

Viewing blends on-screen

6. If you want to see your blends rendered on-screen without banding, you can check the Accurate Blends box in the General Preferences dialog under the Edit menu. ☼: *Your screen will redraw more slowly when the Accurate Blends option is checked.*

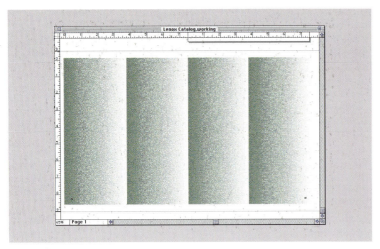

Repeating patterns

7. Repeating the linear blend for each colum in the two-page spread was a subtle and elegant way for Lehner and Whyte to incorporate the four-column grid into their page design.

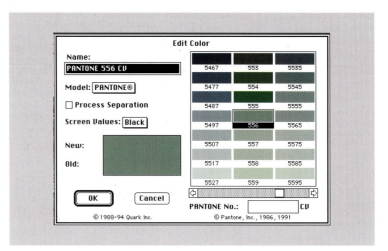

Simulating metallic inks

8. The final printed piece featured a light green metallic ink, which Lehner & Whyte simulated in their electronic document by selecting a Pantone spot color in the Edit Color dialog box under the Edit menu. They then worked with the printer to choose the actual metallic ink that would be used as a fifth color when the catalog was on press. ☀ *You can't specify and separate metallic colors in QuarkXPress so your best bet is to create a close approximation of the color that will act as a placeholder during production.*

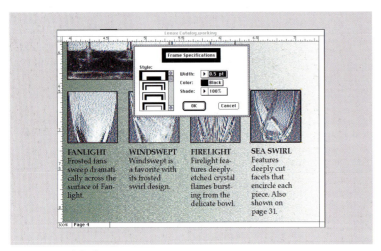

Creating subtle frames

11. Because the product photographs contained strong contrasts from dark to light, and because they would be placed against a background that also ranged from dark to light, Lehner & Whyte created a thin (.5 pt.) frame around each picture using XPress' Frame Specifications dialog (under the Item menu).

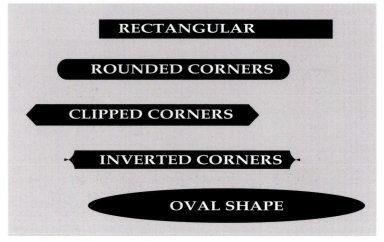

Reversing headlines out of black text boxes

12. In previous versions of QuarkXPress, Lehner & Whyte would have had to place a text box over a black picture box to create the above effects. With the ability to create variable-shaped text boxes in version 3.3, they could easily reverse their type out of any of the above text boxes. For the catalog, they wisely chose the simple rectangular shape (top) to headline each Lenox collection. 🎨 *Just because a feature is available in QuarkXPress doesn't mean it would work well in your design.*

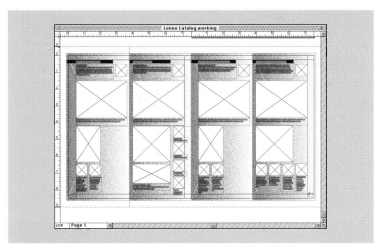

Organizing information

9. One of the biggest challenges in most catalog design is how to present large amounts of information and graphics in an organized fashion. Lehner & Whyte stuck closely to their four-column grid format, neatly grouping pictures and captions within each column. *Grouping elements tightly together with larger gaps left over for white space, rather than spacing elements symmetrically across a page, is one way to create a more inviting layout.*

Using scanned photographs

10. Lehner & Whyte used low-resolution FPO (For Position Only) scans during production of the catalog. The original photographs, used previously in several different Lenox catalogs, were rescanned by the printer to achieve the highest possible quality and consistency. *Another option would be to have your service bureau or color house scan the photographs into Kodak's Photo CD format; this would require processing the photographs through a program such as Adobe Photoshop, however, to adjust contrast levels and the like.*

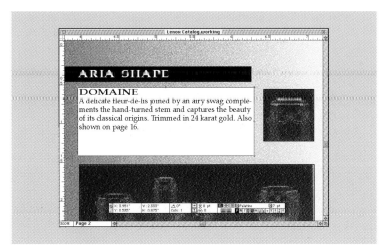

Choosing a typeface

13. Lehner & Whyte chose to use Palatino for both captions and headlines throughout the catalog. The typeface's large x-height and delicate serifs made the text both readable and elegant-looking. Above you can see the XPress Measurements palette as it reflects the text specifications for the selected text box.

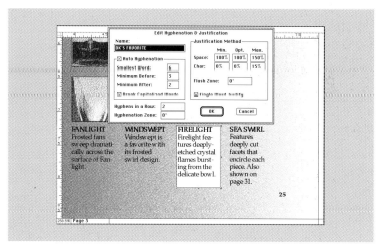

Specifying hyphenation and justification

14. You can create custom hyphenation and justification settings through the H&Js command under the Edit menu. Lehner & Whyte used the above settings, which allowed them to specify such things as the smallest word that could be automatically hyphenated, the minimum number of letters before and after a hyphen, and how many hyphenated words in a row could appear at the end of a line.

6

Specifying Colors for a Four-Color Cover

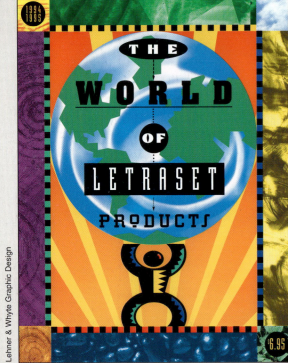

Lehner & Whyte Graphic Design

Illustrators Hugh Whyte and Donna Lehner of Lehner & Whyte Graphic Design created this vibrant cover for their client's 290-page product catalog.

Creating an earth-like image

1. Lehner & Whyte wanted to use bright, earthy colors for the cover of the catalog. They also wanted to use a circular earth shape as the centerpiece of the design. This color Phototone image of swirling water was the perfect background for the earth.

Cropping a photographic image

2. Lehner & Whyte simply imported the Phototone image into a circular picture box. *To reshape an oval picture box (or text box) into a circle, hold down the Shift key while dragging a handle. This technique can also be used to reshape a rectangular box into a square.*

Creating an abstract globe

3. They created this abstract-looking artwork in Adobe Illustrator and placed it into the same size circular picture box.

Layering imges

4. They then placed the picture box containing the land over the photo of the water. *To select an item that is behind another item, press Command Option Shift while clicking. Each click will select the next layer behind the one you just clicked.*

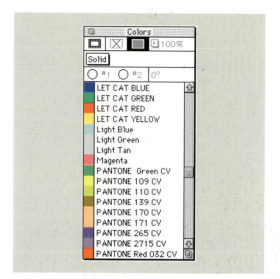

Specifying colors

6. Although the final films were output using process color, Lehner & Whyte used some Pantone colors in the early stages of their design. ☀: *When you import an EPS image into an XPress document, the colors from that image will automatically show up in the Colors palette.*

Trapping

7. You'll notice that this book contains almost no information on how to use XPress trapping. Although you can specify trapping values in XPress (above), we recommend you let your printer take care of trapping, as do all of the designers featured in this book.

Using illustration as background

5. Lehner & Whyte also created this illustration of a sunburst in Adobe Illustrator. In choosing the color scheme for the catalog cover, they wanted a strong balance of blues and yellows. They accomplished that by placing the blue-green globe against this warm yet bright background illustration, which was saved and imported as an EPS image.

Using more four-color photography

9. Lehner & Whyte rounded out their design by importing the following photographic images, chosen for their color and texture. Above is a Phototone image called "Growth Rings."

Colorizing black-and-white TIFF images

8. The above images, which Lehner & Whyte used as the four borders of the catalog cover, were originally black-and-white TIFF images from the Letraset Backgrounds & Borders collections. They colorized them in XPress by first creating the colors via the Pantone Process guide in the Edit Colors dialog box, then assigning the colors to the image via the Colors Palette. ☀: *If you create colors with no QuarkXPress document open, those colors will appear on the Colors palette of subsequently created XPress documents.*

Resizing images

13. Lehner & Whyte created this little "man" in Adobe Illustrator, and used him to hold up the image of the globe. ☀: *To fit a picture exactly into its picture box as shown above, press Command Option Shift and F while the picture is selected with the content tool.*

10. This image, used in the lower-right corner of the catalog cover, is another Phototone image called "Seedlings."

11. Like fitting together the pieces of a puzzle, Lehner & Whyte used this Phototone image, called "Stratus Clouds," in the upper right corner of the cover.

🎨 *Process colors (CMYK) and spot colors are generally specified for printed output, while RGB colors are used for video displays and film recorder output.*

12. They used this image, called "Orange/Red Waves," to again balance out the blue and green tones. 🔧 *To simultaneously resize both a picture box and its contents, first make sure the content tool is selected. Then press Command, Option, Shift, wait a moment for the picture to redraw, and press and drag one of the handles.*

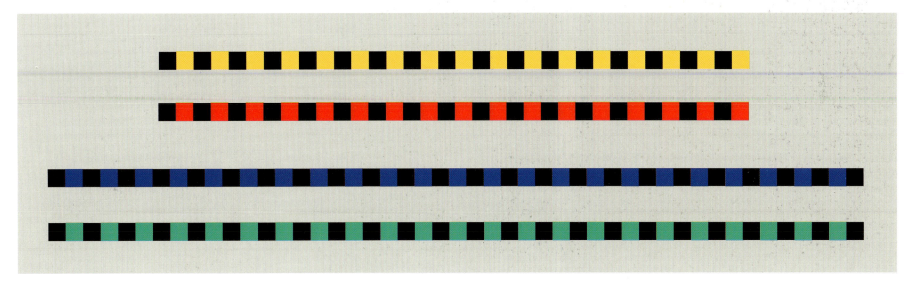

The final touch

14. Primary colors red, yellow, and blue—plus green—were combined with black to create these checkered borders around the central image of the globe and the man. Each checkered box is its own picture box, repeated using XPress' Super Step and Repeat dialog (under the Item menu).

7

Creating a Four-Color Brochure

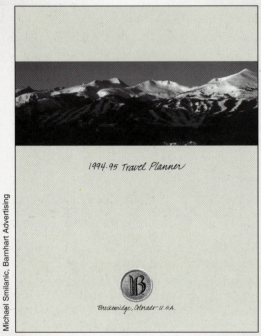

1994.95 Travel Planner

Breckenridge, Colorado · U.S.A.

Michael Smilanic, Barnhart Advertising

Graphic Designer Michael Smilanic of Barnhart Advertising used style sheets and master pages to design this 20-page, four-color brochure, called a Travel Planner, for Breckenridge Ski Corporation of Colorado.

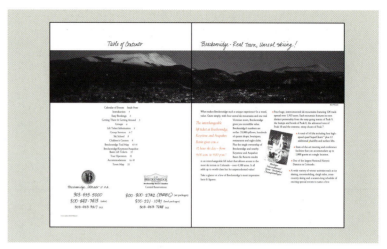

Setting up a format

1. The 1994-95 Travel Planner for Breckenridge, Colorado included a calendar of events, trail maps and a town map, lift ticket and ski school information, hotel and tour listings, plus some stunning four-color photography of mountain scenery. You can get an idea of the format of the entire brochure by glancing across the inside spreads shown on these two facing pages.

Highlighting the mountain scenery

4. Fortunately, Smilanic had access to many stunning four-color photographs which he strategically placed across spreads and on single pages. The photos shown here are black-and-white FPO (For Position Only) TIFF images.

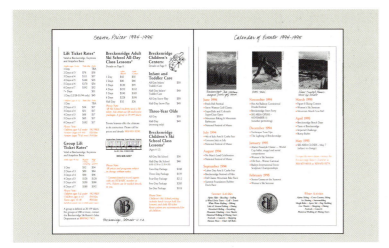

Organizing tabular information
2. Smilanic needed to organize a great deal of tabular information, such as prices and dates, within the brochure.

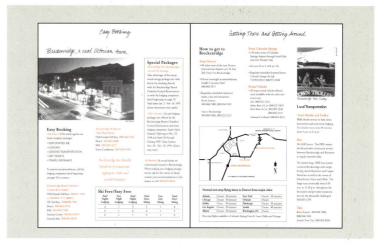

Presenting charts and maps
3. He also needed to incorporate charts and maps throughout the brochure.

Adding other types of artwork
5. To show the breadth of the Breckenridge ski areas, Smilanic used this TIFF image of the eight mountains, three resorts, and 276 trails available to Breckenridge skiers.

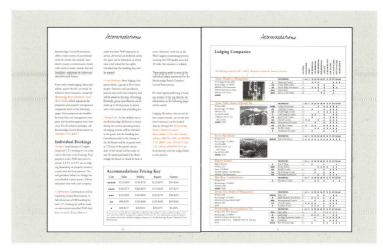

Adding variety to text
6. Smilanic used red type for subheads and other important information as one way to break up the large amount of text in the brochure. He also used dingbats as part of the extensive six-page hotel listings (starting on the righthand page, above) in the back of the brochure.

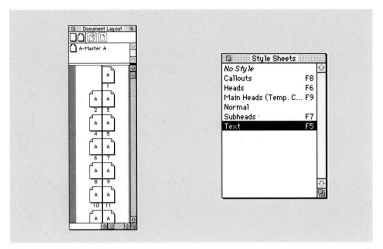

Laying the foundation

7. Two key elements in any type of lengthy document creation (books, magazines, booklets, and long brochures) are making use of XPress' master pages (shown at the top of the Document Layout palette, left) and style sheets (right). Both facilities let you establish continuity while also speeding up production. *QuarkXPress lets you include up to 127 master pages and 127 style sheets per document.*

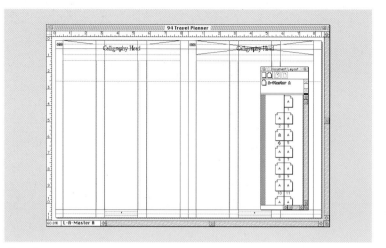

Creating master pages

8. After double-clicking on the master page "A" in the Document Layout palette (provided by default in any new XPress document), Smilanic was presented with two facing pages (specified previously in the Document Setup dialog under the File menu) to which he began applying text boxes.

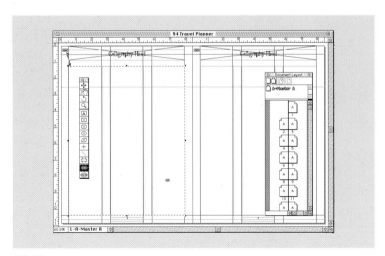

Linking text

11. Because most of the text would be imported via one long Microsoft Word document, Smilanic linked the text boxes on the master pages by clicking on a text box, then clicking on the linking tool (second from bottom on Tool palette), and clicking on the next text box on the facing page. *Each QuarkXPress spread can contain only one automatic text chain. Other boxes on the page can be linked to boxes on the same page, but not across the spread.*

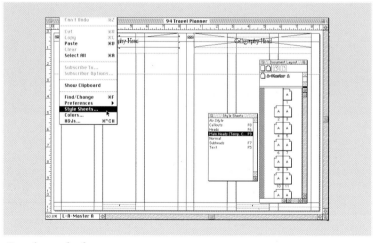

Creating style sheets

12. Smilanic then began the task of creating a style sheet for the Breckenridge brochure by choosing the Style Sheets command under the Edit menu.

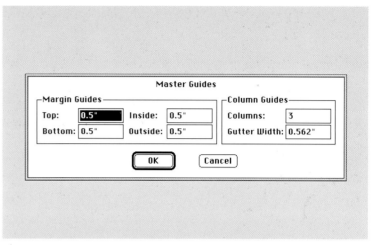

9. For each large text box on the two facing pages, he specified three columns across with a little more than a half-inch gutter between each column using the Text Box Specifications dialog from the Modify command (Command M) under the Item menu. *The zero Text Inset value in the bottom left field speci-fies how closely the text will be positioned to the edges of the text box.*

10. Smilanic could have also modified the margin guidelines and column guides on the master pages using the Master Guides dialog found under the Page menu (accessible only when master pages have been opened). *If you modify master page guides after you've begun laying out your pages, all pages to which that master page have been applied will be changed to show the new guides.*

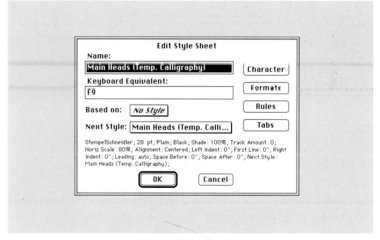

13. Once Smilanic received the Style Sheets dialog box, he selected the style he wished to edit and clicked the Edit button. (Smilanic was simply editing an existing style sheet from last year's brochure.) *Brand new style sheets would contain only the Normal style; you can add completely new styles by clicking the New button instead of the Edit button.*

14. He then received the Edit Style Sheet dialog, which allowed him to enter a name for the style sheet, a keyboard equivalent, and to specify whether or not the new style was based on an existing style. To specify Character Attributes, Paragraph Formats, Rules, and Tabs, he clicked on the corresponding button on the right to receive the necessary dialog boxes.

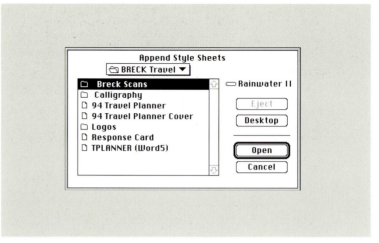

15. Smilanic clicked on the Character button to receive this dialog box, in which he specified his font, size, color, shade, scaling, tracking, baseline shift, and styles such as plain, bold, or italic. Here you can see the Character Attributes for the Main Heads, which are set in 15-point Stempel Schneidler and colored red. Smilanic continued the same process for each style. 🎨 *Although it seems tedious and time-consuming at first, using style sheets for formatting text will save you loads of time in the long run and ultimately make your publication look more clean and neat.*

Appending style sheets

16. ☀: *You can append style sheets from Microsoft Word versions 3.0 and above to QuarkXPress documents using the Microsoft Word filter included with the program.*

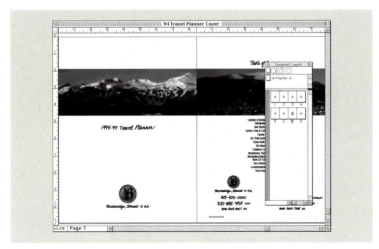

Laying out the pages

19. Smilanic created two separate documents for the Breckenridge brochure: The first document, shown above and in the Document Layout palette, included the front and back covers of the brochure plus a gatefold comprising the inside front covers and the Table of Contents. The second document contained the rest of the inside pages of the brochure.

Placing photography

20. Photos such as the above shot of the Rocky Mountains (used on the cover) were scanned as low-res black-and-white FPO images which Smilanic used to lay out his document and create comps for the client. The actual four-color photos were stripped in conventionally by the printer. 🎨 *You can type the letters "FPO" into a text box and save it as a Quark library. When you want to indicate that an image is For Position Only, simply drag the FPO text box from the Library palette and place it over your image.*

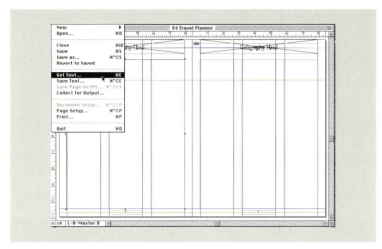

Importing text

17. With style sheets in place and a text box selected, Smilanic began importing text onto his blank pages by using the Get Text command (Command E) under the File menu. ☀: *The same menu command will read Get Picture when a picture box is selected.*

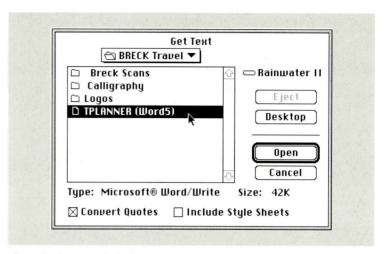

18. In the Get Text dialog box, Smilanic selected the Microsoft Word file to be imported into the Breckenridge brochure. He clicked the Convert Quotes button to convert straight quotes to typographer's quotes.

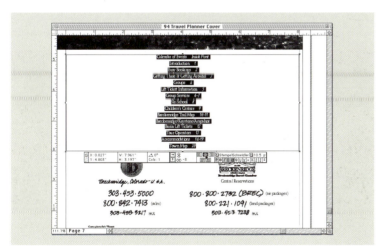

Creating a brief Table of Contents

21. The Table of Contents listing was brief, so Smilanic was able to center the text within its text box by simply selecting it and clicking on the center box of the Horizontal Alignment field in the middle right of the Measurements palette. ☀: *To modify horizontal alignment using the keyboard, select the text, and press Command Shift "L" for flush left text, Command Shift "C" for centered text, Command Shift "R" for flush right text, and Command Shift "J" for justified text.*

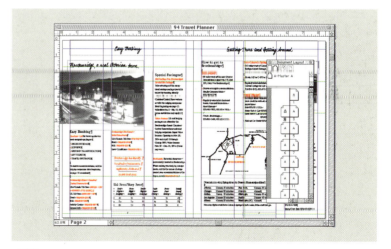

Adding pages

22. As the brochure began to take shape, Smilanic added more pages by simply dragging the master page icon from the top of the Document Layout palette to the bottom of the palette. ☀: *You can also insert pages in the middle of other pages by simply dragging master pages or document pages and dropping them in between the page icons of where you want them to appear.*

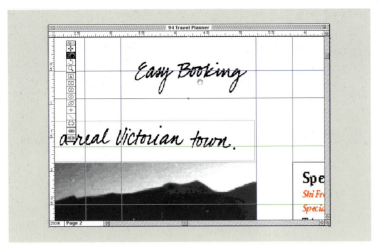

Importing text as graphics

23. Although it looks like text, the calligraphy used in the Breckenridge brochure is actually a number of TIFF files that were created by scanning handwritten text drawn by a calligrapher. Above you can see the grabber hand underneath the words "Easy Booking," which signifies that the contents of the box is a graphic rather than text. ☀ *Had the contents of the box been text, the grabber hand would instead appear as the text cursor. (Both the cursor and the grabber hand appear within the content tool icon, which is second from the top in the Tool palette on the left side of the screen.)*

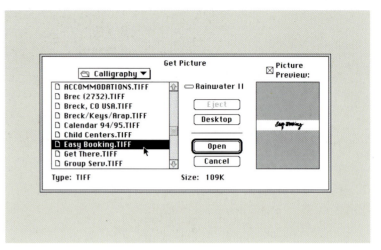

24. With the picture box selected, Smilanic simply pressed Command E (Get Picture) to receive the above dialog box. You can see a preview of the TIFF file on the right of the dialog box.

Using dingbats as bullets

27. Smilanic used the triangular shaped Zapf dingbats colored red for bulleted lists. Using the Baseline Shift command, he raised the baseline of the dingbats by 1 point so they would be vertically centered with the following text.

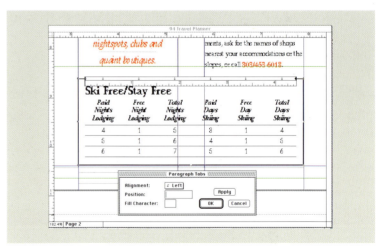

Creating tables

28. QuarkXPress doesn't include any automatic table-creation facility, so Smilanic specified custom tabs via the Paragraph Tabs dialog under the Style menu (Command Shift T) to create the many small tables featured in the brochure. After selecting the text to which the tabs would apply, he selected left alignment from the Alignment pop-up menu and clicked in the tabs ruler (which appears automatically with the Paragraph Tabs dialog) for each custom tab stop. ☀ *You can also enter numeric tab stops via the Position field in the Paragraph Tabs dialog box.*

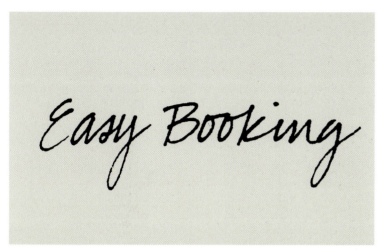

25. Here's a closeup of the calligraphic headlines commissioned especially for Barnhart Advertising.

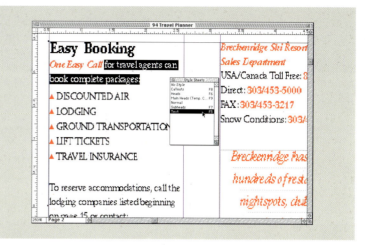

Applying styles
26. With the text flowed and many of the graphics in place, Smilanic began applying the styles from the Style Sheets palette. Above you can see the style "Text" selected and how it appears in the brochure. 👁 *You can apply a style to selected text by clicking on the name of the style in the Style Sheets palette, or by pressing a previously assigned function key when the appropriate text is selected.*

Designing unique callouts
29. In addition to coloring his callouts red, Smilanic applied a subtle dotted line in between each line of text via the Paragraph Rules' Rule Above feature. So that no rule appeared above the first line of text, he simply cut off the rule at the very top of the callout by lowering the top edge of the text box enough to cover up the first Rule Above. 🎨 *Callouts, or pull quotes, are a great way to draw the reader into the text. (They also help take up extra space on a page if you can't figure out what else to do with it.)*

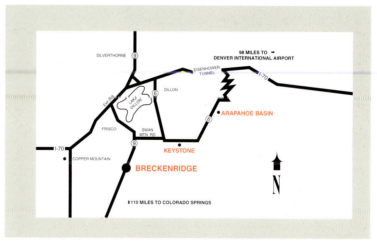

Incorporating maps
30. These maps, which were created in Adobe Illustrator and saved as EPS files, were peppered throughout the brochure to make the Travel Planner even more useful and to give it a longer shelf life.

Colorizing Black-and-White TIFF images

Black-and-white TIFF images can be colorized in QuarkXPress using one-, two-, or three-color tints to simulate the richness of four-color images, while also saving money and disk space. The background for this opening page brochure spread is a black-and-white TIFF image that was colorized using a three-tint combination.

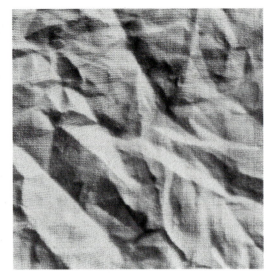

Starting with a low-res TIFF
1. Designer Dermot Mac Cormack of Marcolina Design started with a black-and-white, low-resolution TIFF image called "Linen" from Letraset's Backgrounds & Borders Realities collection of textures, patterns, and shapes.

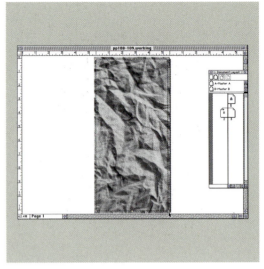

Creating a bleed
2. In order to make sure that the background image for the opening page of the catalog would bleed off the edges of the facing pages, Mac Cormack positioned the low-res TIFF image so that it slightly overlapped the edges of his QuarkXPress document.

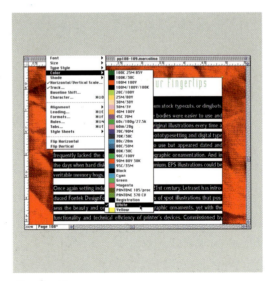

Knockout type
6. To create the reverse type for the body text, Mac Cormack specified the color white through the Color submenu under the Style menu.

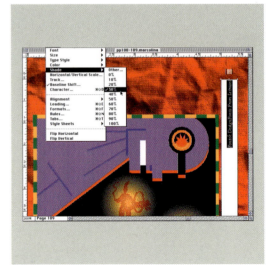

Delicate typefaces
7. To minimize broken letterforms, the delicate type used in the brochure's folios (Figural Book Italic set at 8 points for the text and 14-pt. Mekanik for the page numbers) was given a 30% shade and knocked out of only one of the screens.

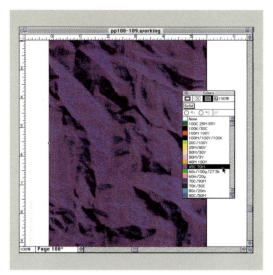

Choosing colors

3. Using a Pantone® CMYK book to calculate the percentages of the process colors, Mac Cormack experimented with different color combinations on-screen. His 13-inch E-Machines monitor is calibrated against Matchprint proof output.

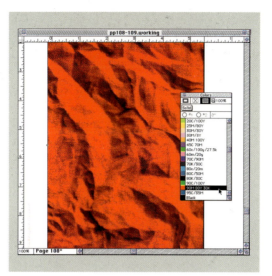

4. He ultimately decided upon a 90% Magenta, 80% Yellow, and 30% Black which he added to his Colors palette and assigned to the black-and-white TIFF image by clicking on the color in the palette and dragging the square color icon to the picture box.

Type considerations

5. One of the primary considerations in choosing his color combinations was the white body type that would be knocked out of the colored background. *Be sure to choose a dark enough background color that will contrast with any light-colored type.*

Sturdy typefaces

8. The more sturdy type used in the brochure's head-lines (Heliotype set at 22 points) was knocked out of two of the background screens and shaded 50%.

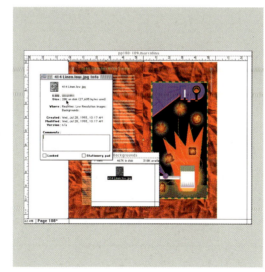

High-resolution vs. low-resolution

9. Because the TIFF file was available in both high-res (266 dpi) and low-res (72 dpi) formats, Mac Cormack used the low-res version during comping to make the file more manageable. (The low-res file was only 28K, while the high-res file was nearly 7MB.)

Updating the low-res TIFF images

10. Using laser proofs that indicated which low-res files should be replaced with high-res files, the printer used QuarkXPress' Picture Usage dialog to update the images before going to film. *All of the color information assigned to the low-res images remains intact.*

Creating One-Color Brochures with Order Forms

Michael Diehl and Paul Volk

DIEHL.VOLK
[typographics]

9**2**

DIEHL VOLK
TYPOGRAPHICS
SPRING 1991

Designers Mike Diehl and Paul Volk created these one-color brochures to promote and sell their type-face designs, created as a collaborative effort through their company, Diehl.Volk Typographics.

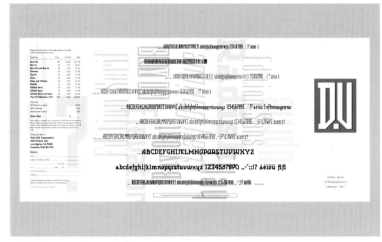

Deciding on size and dimensions

1. The two driving forces behind the design of Diehl and Volk's first brochure was that it be inexpensive to produce and that, when folded, it would fit into a #10 envelope. It was also important to incorporate an order form (shown on the lefthand side of the above image) that recipients of the brochure could easily tear off and place into a return envelope.

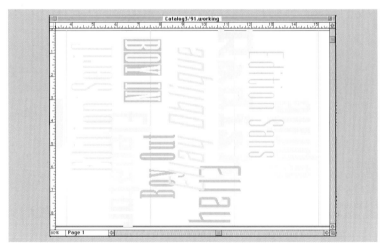

Adding graphic interest with text effects

4. To make the type sampler portion of the brochure more graphically interesting and to show off some of the typographic effects that can be achieved with all of the Diehl.Volk typefaces, Diehl created this background design, which includes the type set at large sizes and shaded at various percentages.

Screening typographic and graphic elements in a one-color brochure will make your design appear more "colorful."

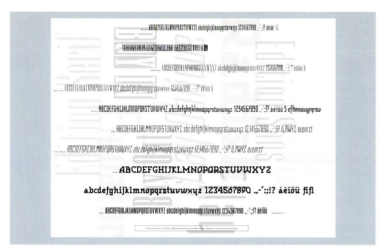

Advertising their product

2. Another important design consideration was that the format of the brochure needed to lend itself to full showings of the Diehl.Volk typeface collection, above. A horizontal format with an extra-long paper width (18.75 inches) that would be folded accordion-style fit their needs perfectly.

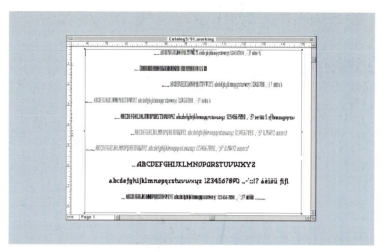

3. Diehl began the brochure design with the most important elements: typesetting the ten Diehl.Volk typefaces at 24 points with 55 points of leading, in order to give the typefaces room to breathe, so they could be viewed as separate units by the reader.

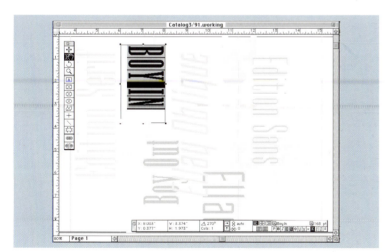

5. Here you can see the content tool is highlighted in the QuarkXPress Tool palette (upper left) while the typeface "Boy In" is selected. You can also see the type specifications in the Measurements palette (bottom of screen): the position of the text box, its dimensions, a 270-degree rotation, auto leading, the name of the typeface, and its point size set at 168 points.

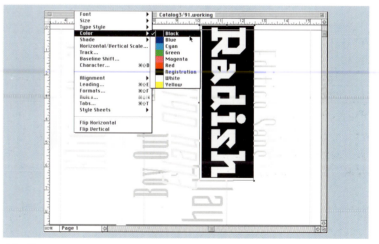

Shading text

6. To make the background text lighter so as not to interfere with the type samples that would appear over it, Diehl individually shaded each text box. After selecting the type with the content tool, he then selected Color (under the Style menu), and chose Black from the submenu.

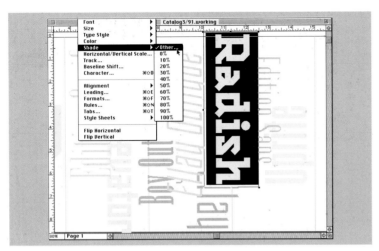

7. With the text still selected, Diehl next selected Shade (also under the Style menu), and chose Other from the Shade submenu.

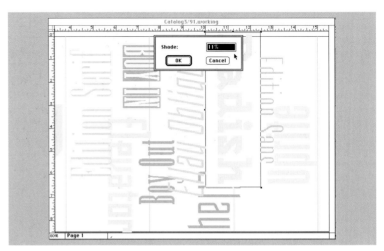

8. Selecting Other from the Shade submenu caused this dialog box to appear, into which Diehl typed 11% for this particular text. The lightest shade he used so that the text would still be visible when printed was 9%, while the darkest shade he used was 25% so as not to interfere with the 100% black text appearing over the screened background. *You can also colorize and shade selected text from the Colors palette.*

Typesetting order forms

11. If you hope to generate direct sales from any type of brochure design, your best bet is to include an order form instead of just the usual address and phone information. The above forms are from the first two Diehl.Volk brochures. *While forms design may seem boring on the surface, the ability to design a functional, good-looking order form can make the distinction between a good designer and a great designer.*

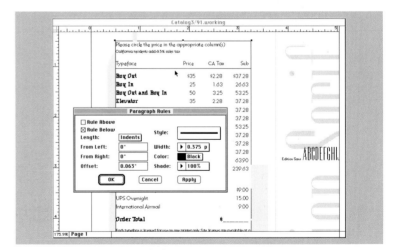

Creating an attractive underline

12. Diehl used XPress' Rule Below feature to creat the thin underline that appears beneath the headings of the order form. He first selected his headlines with the content tool, then pressed Command Shift N to bring up the Paragraph Rules dialog box, and clicked on the Rule Below box. He specified how many fractions of an inch he wanted the underline to appear below the text (Offset) and then specified the width and color of the rule. *You can also incorporate Rules Above and Rules Below into style sheets for lengthier documents.*

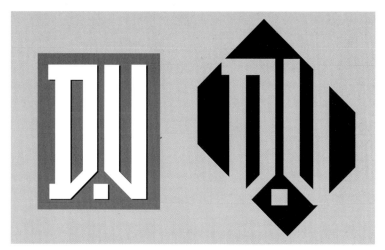

Using two different logos

9. The Diehl.Volk logo on the left was used on the cover of the first brochure, while the logo on the right was used for the cover of Diehl.Volk Typographics' second brochure a year later. Although they are different, the logo designs are similar enough to continue the corporate identity. They were created in FreeHand and saved as EPS images before being imported into the QuarkXPress document.

A closeup of the first Diehl.Volk typefaces

10. Diehl had originally designed the "Boy In" typeface by hand for a series of music CD packaging. It was rendered by a typositor and is still probably available on a strip of film somewhere. The typeface was digitized in FontStudio after Diehl met his partner, Paul Volk, through electronic mail on CompuServe. They then created "Boy Out" and the rest of the Diehl.Volk type library.

Using tabs in forms design

13. To align all the pricing information on the form according to decimal points, Diehl simply selected the appropriate text, selected Tabs from the Style menu (Command Shift T), and selected Decimal from the Alignment pop-up menu.

14. Diehl also used the Tabs dialog box to create the lines for the name and address portion of the order form. With the appropriate text box selected, he again pressed Command Shift T to bring up the Paragraph Tabs dialog box, and typed in two underlines in the Fill Character field. Then, whenever he hit the Tab key for that portion of the text, it would fill out the rest of the empty space with an underline. ☀ *With XPress version 3.3, you can type two different characters into the Fill Character field, such as a dot and a space or a hyphen and a space.*

8

Designing a Book Jacket: One

Artfully cropped and colorized photographs helped to evoke a subtle, pastoral mood for this Doubleday book jacket design by New York designer David High. Photography by Barry Marcus.

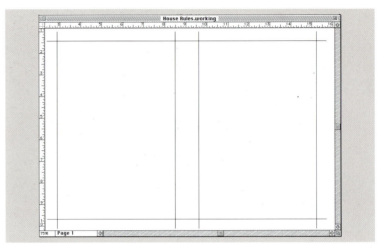

Setting up a grid

1. "Most books are different so I usually start from scratch," says designer David High. He created this grid, outlining the book's front cover, spine, and back cover, using XPress' line tool and Cut and Paste commands, based on specifications provided by Doubleday. *☼ You can also use XPress' non-printing guides to create a grid.*

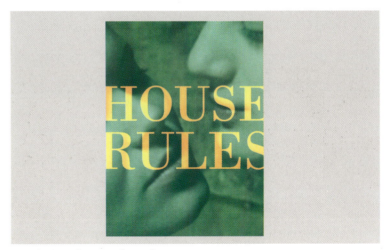

Combining photography and type

3. High created one piece of art by combining a closely cropped photograph and an EPS image of the type (which he created in Adobe Illustrator) in Adobe Photoshop. He scanned the original photograph (which was taken at a photo shoot set up especially for this book jacket) in black and white and converted it to a green duotone in Adobe Photoshop. After adding the EPS image of the type and further manipulating the two in Photoshop, he saved the entire image as a TIFF file to be imported into QuarkXPress.

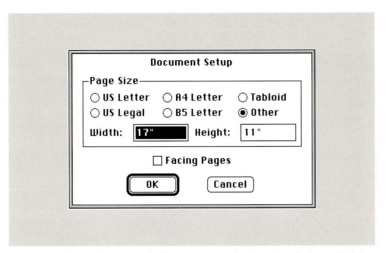

2. High used a single 17 x 11-inch page to contain the entire design, which he specified via the Document Setup dialog box under the File menu.

Adding more photographic imagery
4. Because much of the story took place against the backdrop of the horse-show circuit, High wanted to add some pictures of scenery that were not included in the original photo shoot. He created this picture from a larger painting he found in a local thrift shop, which he scanned using his Umax UC840 scanner.

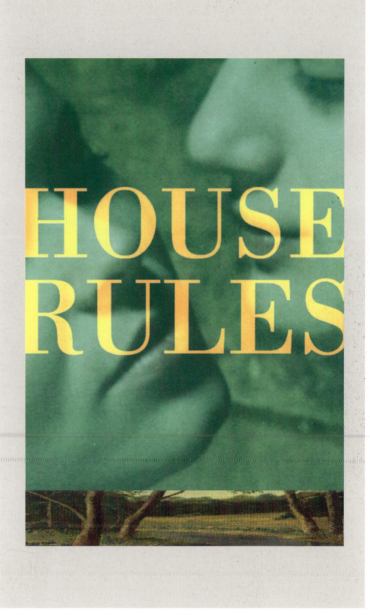

5. He drew a separate picture box at the bottom of the front cover and imported the cropped and stretched TIFF image into QuarkXPress. *He could have also stretched the image directly in XPress by using the Scale Across command in the Modify dialog box (under the Item menu) or the X and Y percentages in the Measurements palette.*

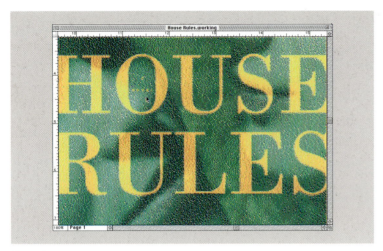

Layering type on type

6. To provide further information about "House Rules" in its cover design, High placed the words "A Novel" in the inside of the "O," where you can see the pointer.

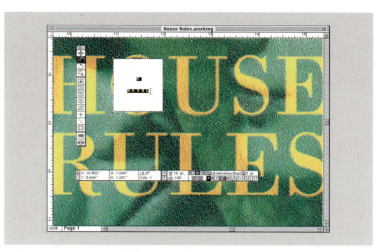

7. He did this by positioning a text box over the "O," and with the content tool selected (see Tool palette on left side of screen), typed in the words, set them in 5-point Helvetica Black via the Measurements palette (bottom of screen), and assigned them a Pantone yellow color via the Colors palette.

Adding the author's name

8. High likes to use a minimum number of typefaces in his jacket designs—usually only two, three at the most. For this book jacket he used Helvetica Black and Bodoni, setting the author's name in the same typeface as the title, Bodoni.

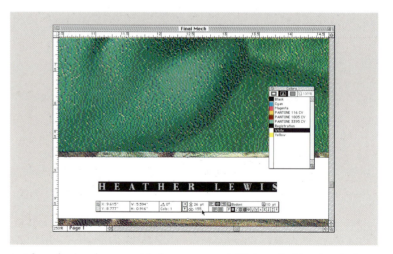

9. After selecting the type with the content tool, High tracked it using the horizontal arrows at the bottom of the Measurements palette, holding down the Option key to track the type in smaller increments. Here he tracked the letters out 155 points. He then colored the type white using the Colors palette so that the type would reverse out of the photographic background.

Combining more photographic imagery

11. This image of a barn door was one of the original photographs from the photo shoot, which High again scanned and saved as a TIFF image.

Creating the back cover

10. Here's a full-size view of the pastoral painting that High found in a thrift store and cropped for the bottom of the front cover. While the image appears in full color on the book's spine, it changes to a blue duotone on the back cover. Each is a separate image placed in its own picture box. High created the blue duotone, above, in Adobe Photoshop. 🎨 *The final version of the book jacket design includes blurbs about the book plus jacket flaps describing the story line, which were added after High submitted his design to Doubleday.*

Cropping

12. After creating a picture box where he wanted the image of the barn door to appear, High imported the TIFF image into his XPress document using the Get Picture command under the File menu (Command E), and with the content tool still selected, moved the image around in its picture box until it was cropped exactly the way he wanted it. Above you can see the grabber hand as it would appear when a picture box is selected with the content tool.

Designing a Book Jacket: Two

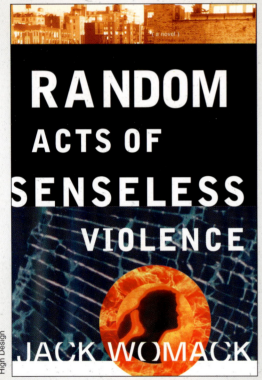

Designer David High created this book jacket design for a novel published by Grove Atlantic, making use of XPress picture boxes for some jarring graphic and typographic effects.

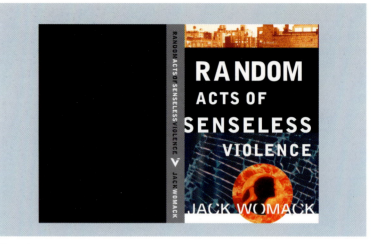

Creating comps

1. "This is the second comp that I created for the book," says designer David High. "The first comp was from a scene right out of the book, which is set in New York in the near future. There's riots on the streets of New York city; all these people are being killed and shards of glass are everywhere. A jet-black limo comes up the street literally driving over bodies, and there's a blood-splattered smiley face on the limo door. My first design was all black with a pixelized·smiley face because they wanted something very cyberpunk, but the publisher has a thing against smiley faces so we had to change it."

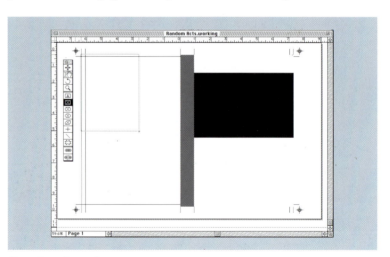

Drawing picture boxes

3. High used the rectangular picture box tool from the tool palette (highlighted in black on left side of screen) to draw the background boxes which served as the foundation for his design.

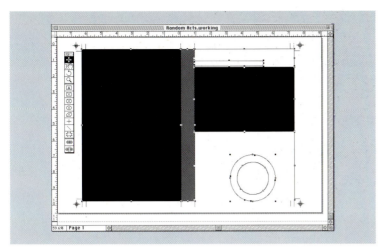

Setting up the document

2. High created the entire book jacket design on a single QuarkXPress page, using the line tool to indicate trim marks and folds, and a dotted line to indicate bleeds. Much of the stark graphic effects were created using simple picture box shapes. 🎨 *Don't forget to assign the Registration color (found in the XPress Colors palette) to all registration and crop marks so that they will appear on all plates.*

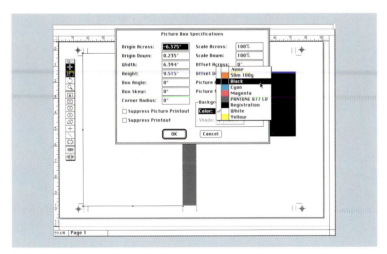

Coloring picture boxes

4. Once the picture box was in place, High used the Modify dialog under the Item menu to change the box's color from white to black. 🔧 *QuarkXPress picture boxes will be automatically colored white unless you specify otherwise.*

Using stock images

5. One of the first things High did upon getting the assignment was to search stock photography catalogs for appropriate images. He specifically wanted images of a cityscape, fire, broken glass, and a girl. The publisher wanted a more electric blue than the original broken glass photograph, so High took the above TIFF image into Adobe Photoshop and intensified the color before exporting it to XPress.

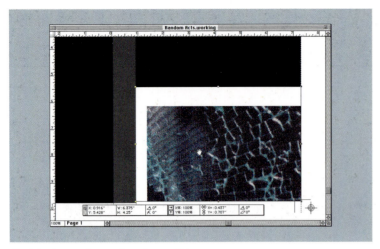

Positioning and cropping the stock images
6. After importing the TIFF image of the broken glass using XPress' Get Picture command (Command E), High used the grabber hand to move the image where he wanted it (shown at 100%—see Measurements palette at bottom of screen).

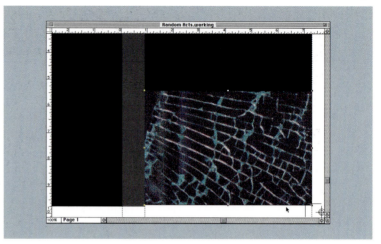

7. Shown here with its picture box selected, High decided that the placement of the broken glass was a bit too symmetrical. In keeping with the story line of the book, he wanted the jacket design to appear somewhat chaotic.

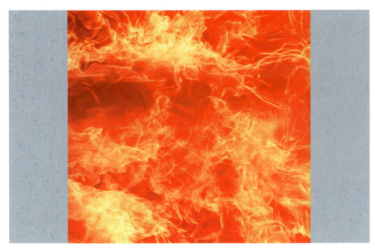

10. Here's the full TIFF image of the fire he used as the ring around the image of the girl.

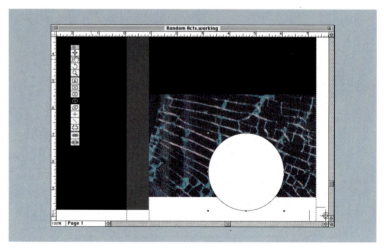

Placing graphics in irregular shapes
11. High used the oval picture box tool (highlighted on the Tool palette at left of screen) to create the circular picture box into which the image of the fire would be imported.

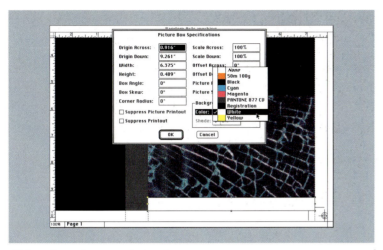

Using picture boxes as design elements

8. To offset the symmetry, High drew a white picture box over the bottom of the broken glass image (bottom of screen) and used the Modify dialog to make sure it was colored white. ☀️: *You can also colorize picture boxes and text boxes from the Colors palette.*

More stock photography

9. High used this cityscape (which he manipulated in Adobe Photoshop) to portray the urban setting of the book, and imported it into his XPress document as a TIFF file.

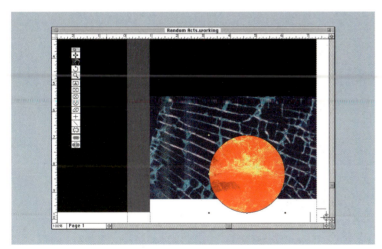

12. With the content tool selected, he pressed Command E and selected the fire TIFF file to bring it into the circular picture box.

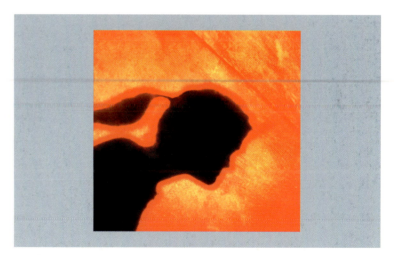

13. The story of "Random Acts of Senseless Violence" is told through the eyes of a young woman who is transformed by the violence that surrounds her and writes about her experiences in her diary. Thus, it was important for High to represent her character through this stock image, which he retouched extensively in Adobe Photoshop.

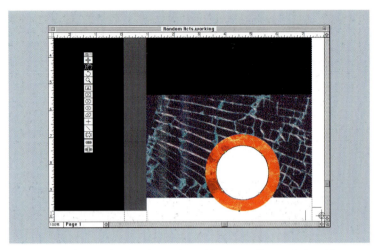

14. He again drew a circular picture box, this one smaller, and placed it over the circular picture box of the fire.

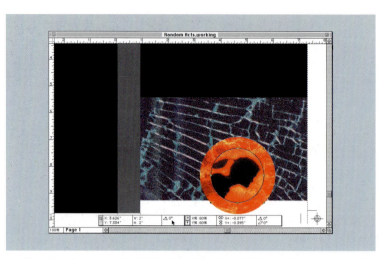

15. High then imported the TIFF file of the girl at 80% into the second smaller circle, but her silhouette was off balance in the original image. Note the zero degrees rotation value in the middle of the Measurements palette.

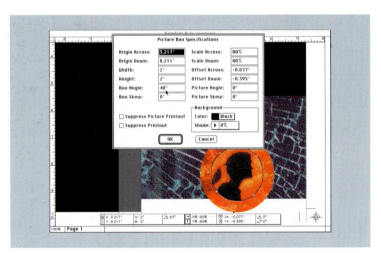

Rotating the silhouette

16. Using the Modify dialog box, High rotated the image 40 degrees.

☼: *You can also rotate text and picture boxes by typing positive or negative values into the Measurements palette and hitting the Return or Enter key, or by using the rotation tool in the Tool palette as described on page 3.*

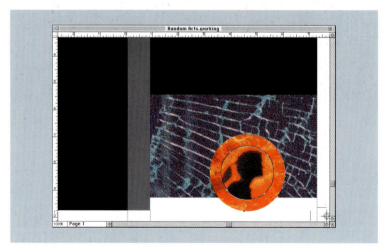

17. High liked the way the ring of fire melded into the "orangey yellowy" colors surrounding the image of the girl.

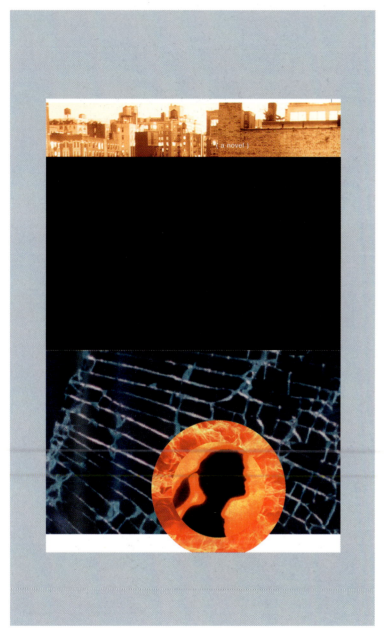

Laying the foundation
18. He had now created a graphic foundation onto which he could begin adding his typographic effects. "Finding the right images was easy," he says. "The type was the hard part."

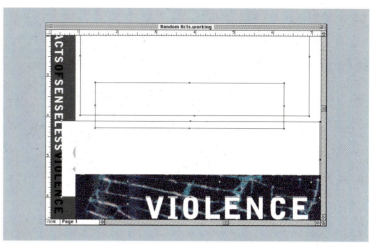

Adding text
19. Instead of importing all of his text into one big text box, High drew individual, overlapping text boxes for each word or group of words so that he would have more control when stylizing each word.

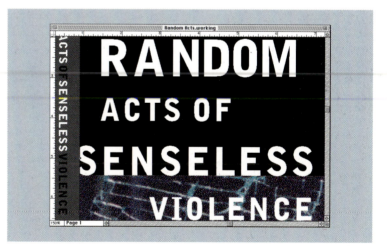

Creating chaos
20. High wanted the type to convey a disorderly feeling to the reader. "The precision of designing on the computer can be a hindrance," he says. "Sometimes I miss the roughness of pasteup."

RANDOM

Unconventional kerning

21. High wanted to continue the disorderly tone set by his graphics with his typography. Although he used only one typeface for the entire jacket design (Bell Gothic Black), he used several typographic techniques to achieve a feeling of chaos—one of which was unconventional kerning. Whereas most designers and typesetters use kerning to achieve a look of symmetry and evenness in display-size type, High purposely kerned the letters in such a way as to make them look more uneven. Above you can see the word "Random" as it appears with no kerning applied whatsoever.

24. Here's the first word of the book title as it appears at its actual size. When High turned in the comp to the publisher, they asked him if he realized that the kerning was off in his headline type. Once he explained that the uneven kerning was intentional and what his logic was, they loved it.

22. After typing the text into his text box, styling it, and sizing it to 120 points, High placed the cursor between the "N" and the "D," the "D" and the "O," and the "O" and the "M" to apply a negative kerning value of minus 20 points. This had the effect of squishing the last four letters together while the first three letters remained farther apart.

Reversing type out of a dark background
23. High then colored the type white by first selecting it, then selecting the boxed letter "A" in the top portion of the Colors palette, and clicking on the word White in the list of colors.

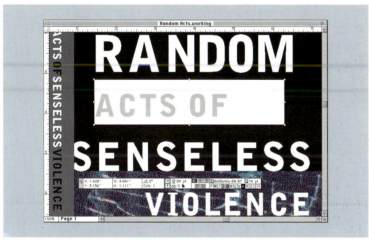

Creating chaos out of order
25. In addition to kerning, High specified different point sizes for each line of text to further add to the chaotic nature of the design.

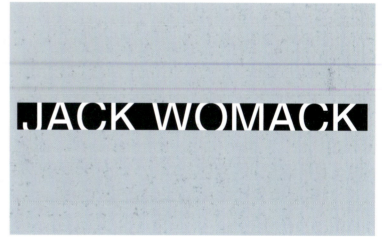

You can't do this in XPress
26. QuarkXPress won't let you cut off the edges of type within a text box. To create the above effect for the author's name, High set the white type in Adobe Illustrator and saved it as an EPS image. He then imported it into an XPress picture box with a black background, and used the edges of the picture box to crop the EPS image.

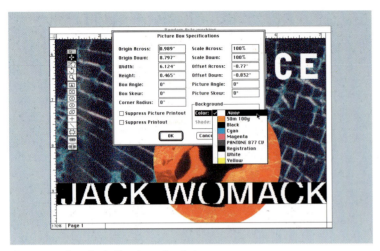

Incorporating the byline into the design

27. High wanted the graphic background to show through the background of the picture box containing the author's name, so he simply changed the background of the box to None via the Modify dialog.

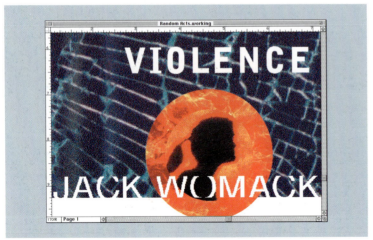

28. The author's name now features the same subtle frame effects as the ring of fire around the girl's silhouette.

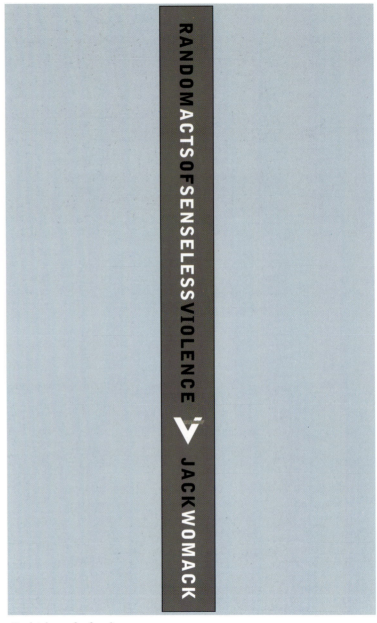

Designing a book spine

29. Although his comp shows a flat gray color for the spine, the final book jacket will be printed in silver.

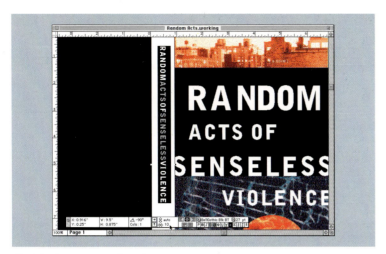

Positioning type on the spine
30. High rotated the text box 90 degrees and tracked the entire book title by 10 points (see Measurements palette). He also removed any spaces between each of the words, and alternately colored each word black and white to make each word distinguishable.

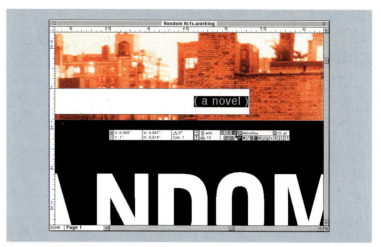

Adding more typographic detail
31. To indicate that the book was a work of fiction, High added a small text box above the title and typed in the lowercase words "a novel." He then used the Measurements palette to flush the type all the way to the right of the text box. *You can also type Command Shift "R" to make the selected text flush right via the keyboard.*

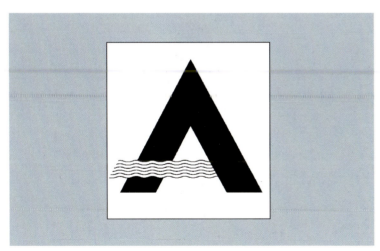

A final touch
32. At the last minute High took Grove Atlantic's logo (above) and turned it upside down (step #33). "Federal Express was at my door ready to take the package, and I just had this idea to turn the logo upside down. I really thought they would hate it," he says.

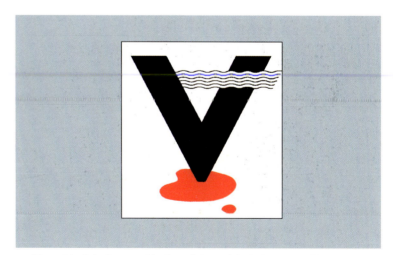

33. "Once I had the logo upside down," says High, "I drew a small pool of blood underneath the logo by cutting out a piece of rubylith and pasting it onto the comp. It's just so over the top—there's a lot of black humor in it, and they ended up leaving it in the design." (Above is the new logo after High recreated it in Adobe Photoshop.)

8

Designing the Interior Pages of a Cookbook

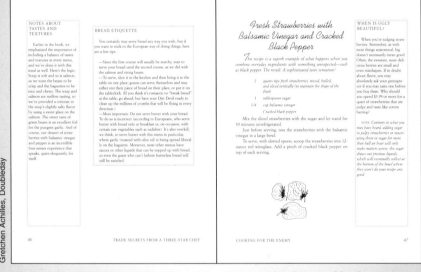

To match the lively and lighthearted writing style of the cookbook's authors, graphic designer Gretchen Achilles provided a light and airy look for the interior pages of Trade Secrets from A Three-Star Chef, *published by Doubleday.*

Creating a mood

1. Looking at the two-page spreads across the top row of boxes, you can see the distinct style in which Gretchen Achilles designed and typeset the interior pages of this cookbook. She needed to incorporate introductory text, lists of ingredients, sidebars, and notes into a free-flowing, yet cohesive format.

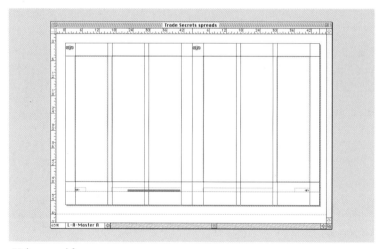

Using a grid

4. Like that of most designers, Achilles' first step was to establish a grid, which she would use throughout the entire book. She began by setting up her master pages as facing pages (Document Setup under the File menu), and specifying three columns across each page with a 1p6 (1 pica, 6 point) gutter between each column in the Master Guides dialog under the Page menu.

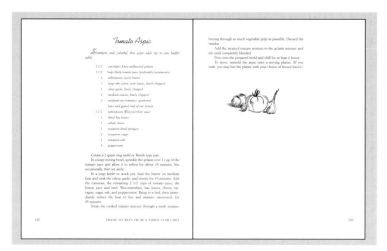

2. Some of the two-page spreads within the cookbook contained just the basics of a recipe—ingredients and instructions (above), while other spreads included a little bit of everything, such as sidebars, lists, notes, and more introductory text, as seen in previous spreads.

3. Still other pages in the cookbook contained a running-text format, with very few graphics (above). Achilles made use of wide outer margins and neatly typeset text to make the most of her page designs.

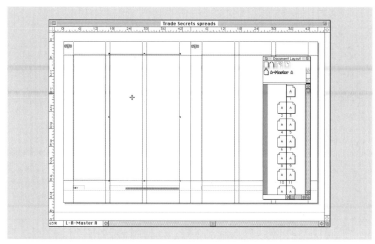

Setting up master page items

5. Achilles used the text box tool to create text boxes on each of her master pages. The outside text box on each page is one column wide, while the inside text box spans two columns (selected with the item tool on the lefthand page, above).

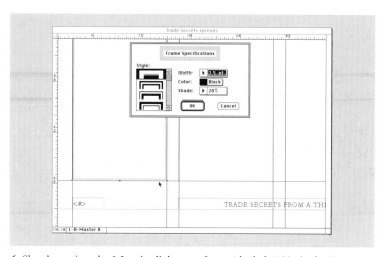

6. She also assigned a 2.5-point light gray frame (shaded 20% via the Frame Specifications dialog, above) to the outside text boxes, which would contain sidebars and notes. *By creating these elements on the master pages, Achilles saved herself a lot of production time. Even if she ended up modifying or deleting a text box, it was much more efficient to change an existing item on each page rather than create one from scratch.*

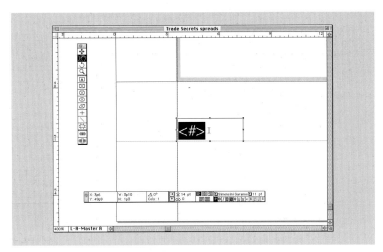

Creating automatic page numbers

7. While still in the master pages, Achilles drew a text box and, with the cursor placed inside the text box, pressed Command 3 to create automatic page numbering for all of the document pages. She added styling directly to the page numbering command (Simoncini Garamond, 11/14) so that all subsequent page numbers would be automatically styled. ☀ *If you add or delete pages to the document using the Document Layout palette when using this command, your page numbers will automatically update. If you enter page numbers manually on each page, they will not automatically update after pagination changes.*

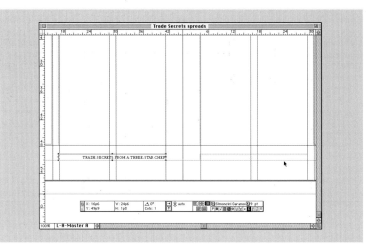

Creating folios

8. Achilles drew text boxes where she wanted her folios to appear. She added the title of the book and set it in 9-point Simoncini Garamond on the lefthand master page, leaving the righthand text box blank for the names of the chapters to be added later.

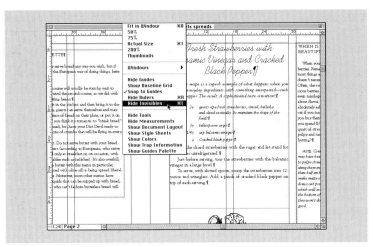

11. She also used Show Invisibles (also under the View menu) to show paragraph returns, spaces, tabs, and other non-printing characters while working on her document (Command I).

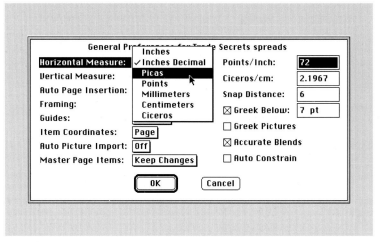

Specifying preferences

12. While many designers in the U.S. work in inches, Achilles likes to use picas as her measurements system. She specified this via the General Preferences dialog box under the Edit menu. ☀ *When entering measurement specifications via the Measurements palette, use the following abbreviations: "P" (picas), pt or "p" followed by a number (points), "cm" (centimeters), "mm" (millimeters), "c" (ciceros), and " (inches/inches decimal). You can combine picas and points by typing "10p6," for example. To produce an inch mark when the Smart Quotes option is enabled, press Control Shift " (or Control ' for foot marks).*

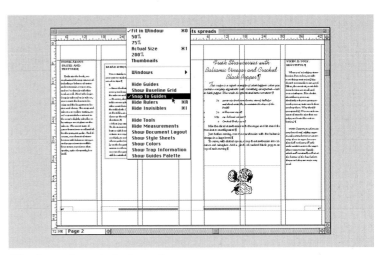

9. Above you can see the master page items as they appear on-screen, including page numbers, folios, text boxes, framed sidebars, as well as master guides.

Viewing and manipulating a document
10. XPress offers several options for working with and viewing your document. Achilles used the Snap to Guides feature under the View menu to make her text and picture boxes snap to the grid.

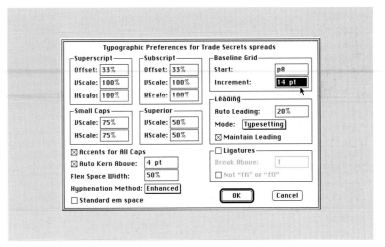

Using a baseline grid
13. In order to neatly align her text throughout the cookbook, Achilles used the Lock to Baseline Grid feature found in the Paragraph Formats dialog box under the Style menu (Command Shift F). ☀ *You can also access this feature when creating and editing Style Sheets (under the Edit menu).*

14. In the Typographic Preferences dialog box (under the Edit menu), Achilles specified a Baseline Increment that was equal to the amount of leading used in most of her text (14 points). ✐ *In order for your baselines to align correctly, you need to use a baseline increment that is either a multiple of or equal to your text leading.*

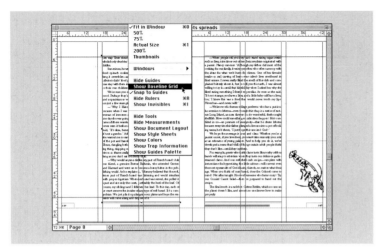

Viewing a baseline grid

15. To see how her text was aligning to the baseline grid, Achilles simply selected View Baseline Grid from the View menu. Above you can see a text-intensive spread without the Baseline Grid showing.

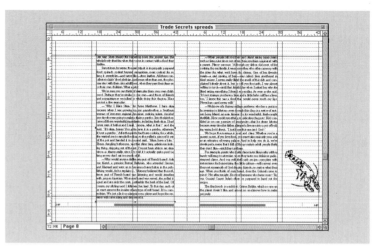

16. Here you can see the same text-intensive spread with the View Baseline Grid option turned on. *Aligning text to a baseline is an important step in designing text-heavy publications such as magazines, books, and newsletters.*

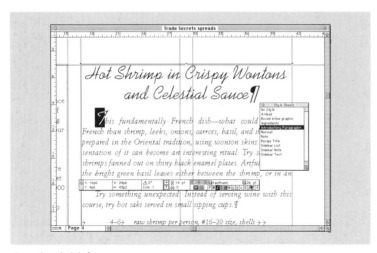

Creating initial caps

19. Although she could have done it automatically with the XPress drop cap feature (in the Formats dialog under the Style menu), Achilles manually created her initial caps by simply styling the first letter of the introductory paragraph. Maintaining the same leading (14-pt.) so that the first line would still align to the grid, she set the initial cap in 26-point Kaufman.

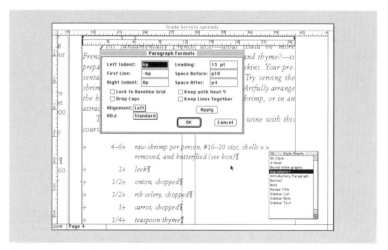

Specifying space before and after lines

20. As part of the style for the ingredients list, Achilles specified a value of 10 points before a line and 4 points after a line in the Space Before and Space After fields of the Paragraph Formats dialog. This allowed her a greater degree of control than simply using paragraph returns to offset each line of text.

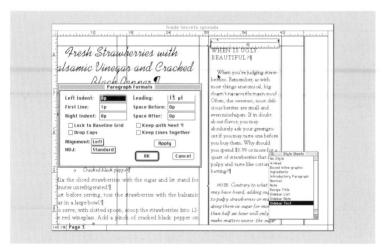

17. Here's a closeup of the body text as it locks to the baseline grid. One of the most important functions of this feature is to align text from column to column and from page to page.

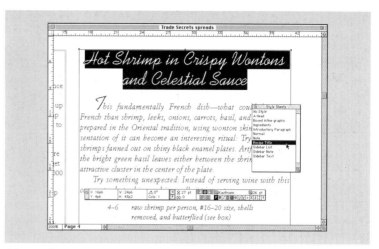

Typesetting text
18. Although she only used two typefaces throughout the entire book (Simoncini Garamond and Kaufman), Achilles made use of an extensive style sheet system to automate the process of typesetting the large amount of text. After selecting her text, she simply clicked on the corresponding style in the Style Sheets palette. ☼: *You can also apply styles using keyboard shortcuts assigned via the Edit Style Sheets dialog under the Edit menu.*

Setting up indents
21. Achilles also specified paragraph indents for each of her styles via the Paragraph Formats dialog. Here you can see the first line of the style called "Sidebar Text" indented 1 point.

Importing graphics
22. Hand-drawn graphics were scanned and saved as TIFF images, then placed throughout the book to add to the warm and lively style of the overall design. ☼: *To resize a picture and its box at the same time, select the content tool, press Command Option Shift, then click and drag any handle.*

Creating
a
CD-ROM Boxed Set

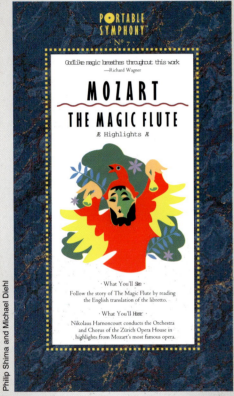

Designers Philip Shima and Michael Diehl created this package design for an entire series of CD-ROMs, called the "Portable Symphony," which featured visual information such as the actual music scores and biographies of the composers as well as audio entertainment.

Designing with precision
1. One of the keys to producing an efficient package design is using correct dimensions and trim sizes right from the start. QuarkXPress' precise measurements system allowed Diehl to easily execute the design for both the front and back of the CD-ROM packaging.

Creating a template
2. Because Warner New Media's CD-ROM packaging often varied in size, Diehl usually had to create a new template for each new package design. He sometimes even recreated electronic templates (above) from film templates created by the color separator.

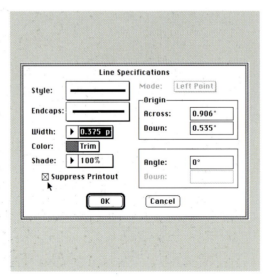

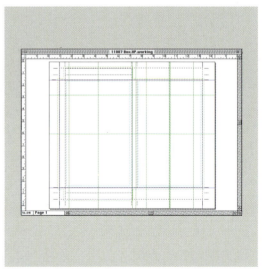

6. While his trim lines were still selected, Diehl pressed Command M to bring up the Modify dialog box under the Item menu, and clicked on the Suppress Printout box so that the lines wouln't show up when the final document was printed.

7. Diehl could now use his template in combination with the Show Guides command (under the View menu)…

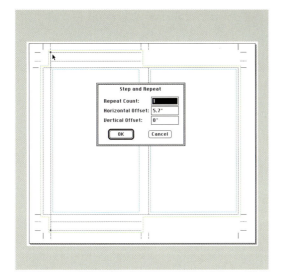

3. In order to place all the crop marks and trim lines with the utmost precision, Diehl used XPress' Step and Repeat command to duplicate horizontal and vertical lines according to the exact height and width of the packaging.

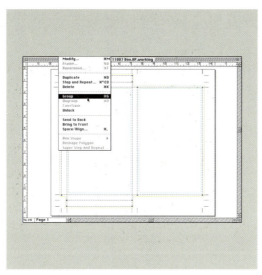

4. He then selected all the trim lines while holding down the Shift key, and grouped them together using the Group command under the Item menu (Command G). ☼: *Grouped items will be surrounded by a dotted line when selected with the item tool.*

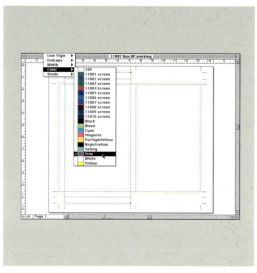

5. Diehl color-codes the lines on his template according to whether they are trim lines, registration marks, or "safety" margins. Here he colored his selected trim lines gray via the Style menu.

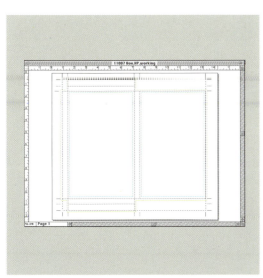

8. ...or without the guides showing (Hide Guides). Either way, he always had a frame of reference for crop marks, trim lines, registration, and folds within his template.

Choosing a background

9. Diehl and Shima searched stationery shops and art stores until they found a handmade marbled paper from France, which was scanned by their separator and saved as a DCS file. What you see above is the FPO image that Diehl used in his XPress file.

10. Diehl then imported the FPO image into his package template using Command E (Get Picture). He then enlarged the image to 105% in the Modify dialog under the Item menu so that it would cover the dimensions of the box.

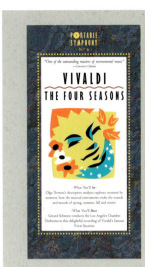

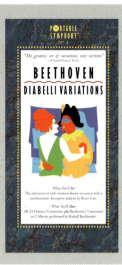
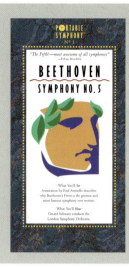
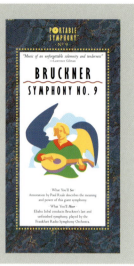

Creating a consistent look

11. Using the marbled background on all ten packages in the series not only helped to achieve a classical look, but also created an easily recognizable format for the entire Portable Symphony series. Diehl and Shima chose to use a scan of an actual handmade paper instead of a stock marbled background to get a larger surface and more variety than could be achieved with using a smaller, repetitive stock image duplicated to fill the background.

Combining classical and modern design

13. Again juxtaposing classical and modern elements, Shima and Diehl used a modern display face, Gill Sans Extra Condensed Bold, to complement Centaur, a classic text face. The wavy line was created in Adobe Illustrator and saved as an EPS (Encapsulated PostScript) image.

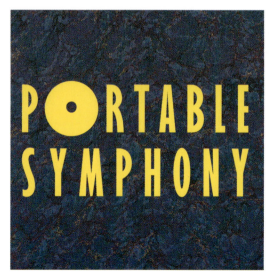

Creating a logo for the series

14. Shima created this logotype in FreeHand and saved it as an EPS file.

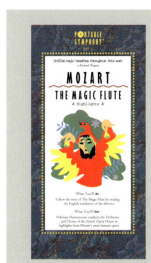

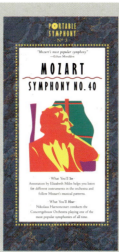

Using modern illustrations

12. Because it was CD-ROM software, Diehl and Shima wanted to juxtapose a modern touch against the classical background. They commissioned these illustrations from Douglas Bevans in England and worked with him via modem and fax.

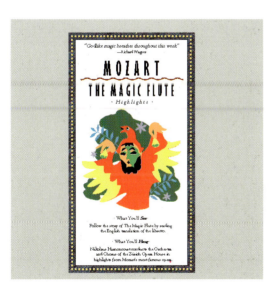

Creating a custom frame

15. Shima used the QuarkXPress Frame Editor to create the dotted yellow line that surrounds the white box on both the front and back of the package.

16. Both Diehl and Shima thought about using XPress-generated rules, but the dotted line style found in the line tool Measurement's palette and the Paragraph Rules dialog (above) featured rounded shapes, not the square boxes they wished to use.

17. They settled on the dotted squares in the Frame Specifications dialog box under the Item menu, and gave it the same custom yellow used for the type.

✦ *XPress frames created with the Frame Editor are bitmapped images—not PostScript—and may not look good when printed.*

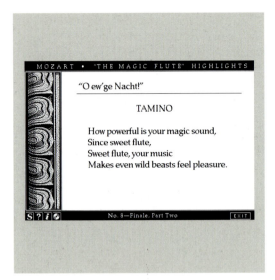

Importing and colorizing screen shots
18. Warner New Media supplied Diehl with black-and-white PICT files showing the CD-ROM interface. Diehl converted the PICT files to TIFF before importing them into his XPress document. ✏: *Try to avoid PICT-format files whenever possible, as they increase your XPress file size and can be difficult to output.*

19. Diehl then assigned a process blue color to the screen shot to make it more visually pleasing.

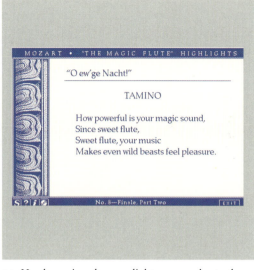

20. He also assigned a very light creme color to the non-colorized portion of the screen shot so that it would blend into the creme-colored background of the back of the packaging.

Creating an automatic drop cap
24. It's easy to create automatic drop caps in XPress: Select a paragraph with the content tool, press Command Shift F, check the Drop Caps box, and specify how many letters you want enlarged and how many lines deep you want them dropped.

More special characters
25. You never know what interesting dingbats, bullets, and symbols you might find contained within a high-quality typeface. Diehl pressed Option 7 to find this symbol in Centaur.

26. He and Shima liked the special character so well they decided to use it for the bulleted copy on the back of the package design. ✺ *You don't always have to use standard bullets, even in conservative designs. Small details such as a nicely designed bullet or paragraph marker can turn a plain design into an extraordinary design.*

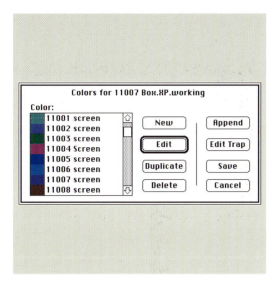

21. Diehl and Shima came up with an entire palette of colors using the Edit Colors dialog (under the Edit menu) for each screen shot that appeared on all the different boxed sets.

Using bullets

22. Although Diehl has been known to design his own bullets when he doesn't like the ones that come with a font, he liked the diamond-shaped bullet that comes with Centaur well enough to use in this package design, as you can see above.

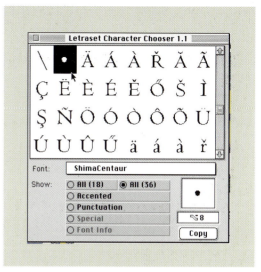

Locating special characters

23. You can use utilities such as Key Caps or the Letraset Character Chooser (above) to help you see the variety of special characters available within a particular font.

Creating peripheral packaging

27. Diehl and Shima also created CD jewel case inserts (above) and inlays to match the entire boxed set.

Applying bar codes

28. Diehl received the previously created bar codes from Warner New Media and placed them in his design as EPS files. Nowadays you can create bar codes on-the-fly with QuarkXPress XTensions *(see page 121 for more details).*

29. *Knowing how to create and properly position bar codes is an especially important skill for package designs, book covers, magazines, and many other commercial projects.*

9

Creating a CD DigiPak

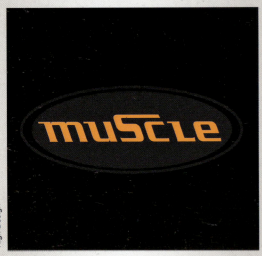

High Design

New York designer David High created this design for a compact disc "DigiPak," which, unlike the traditional CD jewel case, is constructed out of cardboard and includes a plastic tray for the disc. The CD, called "muscle," was put together as a promotional recording by MCA and featured several artists.

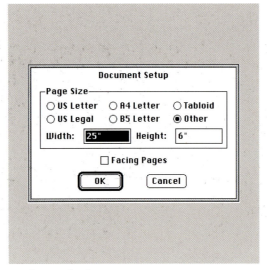

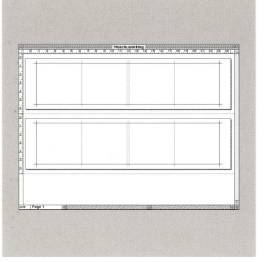

Setting up the document

1. The template for the Muscle CD contained two QuarkXPress pages, each 25 inches wide by 6 inches high, folded according to the package measurements provided by MCA.

2. Here you can see the blank document with which High began his package design. The inside vertical lines represent folds. DigiPaks, as opposed to standard plastic CD jewel cases, are said to be more ecological because they are made primarily of thick cardboard and can be recycled.

4. The above two panels form the inside gatefold of the right side of the DigiPak (shown in step #3), with song titles listed on the right.

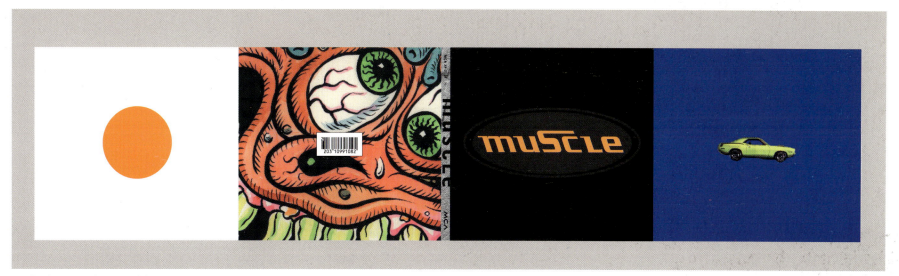

Designing according to folds

3. Here's the design of the outside of the DigiPak, which folds inward at the middle (green vertical spine). The black-and-orange panel is the front of the DigiPak, while the monster illustration appears on the back of the package. The panel on the far left folds inward and rests underneath the plastic compact disc tray, while the panel on the right with the small green car is part of a gatefold (see step #4).

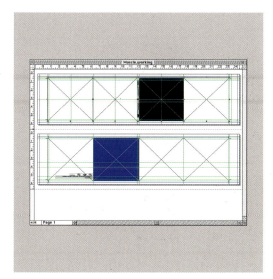

Laying down picture boxes

5. High created picture boxes for each panel using the Step and Repeat command (under the Item menu). He then began adding color to the boxes via the Modify dialog, also under the Item menu.

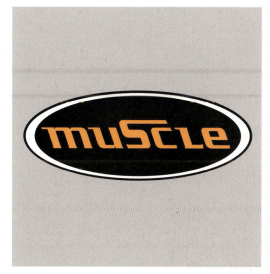

Creating a logo

6. The theme that was established by MCA was '70s muscle cars. Knowing that they wanted to name the disc "muscle," High based his logo design on the familiar shape of STP bumper stickers.

7. He created the logo in Adobe Illustrator, using a sans serif typeface called Serpentine, which he slanted in reverse, and to which he also added serifs. He saved the logo as an EPS image in several different colors to be used in various parts of the packaging.

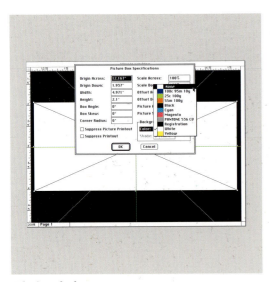

Placing the logo

8. High drew a picture box on the front black panel, then changed its background color to None via the Modify dialog. With the content tool selected, he then imported the black and orange logo into the picture box using Command E (Get Picture).

Special effects with printing

9. You won't see it in the QuarkXPress document, but, when printed, the front of the packaging will feature a high-gloss black for the background and a matte black for the STP-shaped ovals.

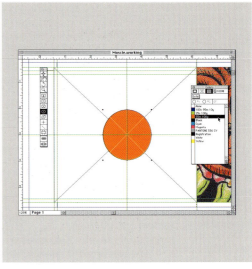

Special effects with packaging

10. This is the panel on which the plastic CD tray will rest. The orange dot, which High drew with the circular text box tool, will show through the starburst-shaped plastic center that holds the disc in place.

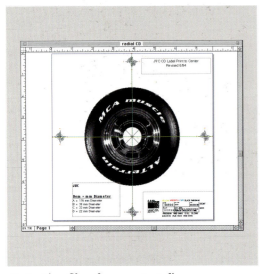

Outputting films for a compact disc

12. MCA provided the XPress template in which High created the file that would contain the design pressed onto the compact disc (above).

13. He learned that the film output of his image would be flipped horizontally, so that when it was pressed back onto the CD, it would appear right side up.

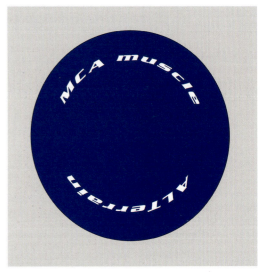

14. High created the white type, which at first glance appears to be part of the mag wheel, in Adobe Illustrator. He placed the rounded picture box containing the type directly over the wheel, and gave it a background of None (via the Modify dialog) so that the wheel would show through. Here the EPS file of the white type is shown against a blue background.

The compact disc

11. You can even use QuarkXPress to create the pattern embedded onto a compact disc. In keeping with the '70s car theme, High imported this TIFF image of a mag wheel into a separate XPress document, which was output to film and pressed onto the CD.

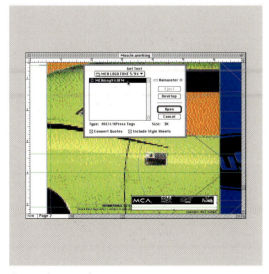

Importing text logos

15. Vital to any package design is the company logo, which was available to High as a text file called "MCA font." He simply imported the MCA logo font into his text box using the Get Text command (Command E).

Finding the right illustration

16. High originally wanted to use a Big Daddy Roth illustration from the "'50s/'60s ratfink gross-out school of illustration" on the back of the CD DigiPak, but time and budget constraints prohibited him from exploring usage rights. Luckily, a friend of one of the MCA executives, Mark Durham, painted the above illustration overnight using watercolors, which High then scanned and saved as a TIFF image.

Using digital barcodes

17. The barcode, which appears on the back panel of the packaging on top of the monster image, was provided to High by MCA as a UPC font. High simply typed in the numbers of the product code, and specified the UPC font via the Measurements palette.

Using art instead of a solid color

18. Instead of simply specifying a solid green color for the narrow spine of the packaging, High drew a vertical picture box into which he imported the electronic image of the car, which was used previously on the inside panels of the DigiPak.

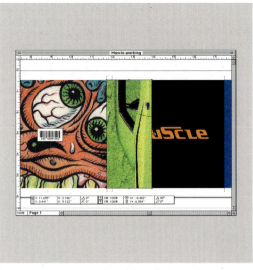

19. Here you can see the widened picture box showing the image of the car, which High had rotated 90 degrees. If you look very closely you can see the cursor turned into a pointing finger as High used one of the handles on the right side of the picture box to make it narrower.

Setting small type

23. High had a lot of song title information he needed to squeeze onto the inside panel, shown above.

24. He at first convinced MCA to omit the really fine print, leaving just the song titles and their artists (above), but later decided the panel needed something more.

Positioning text boxes

25. To give the text its semi-haphazard appearance, High layered individual text boxes. Above you can see the first group of songs selected in their text box, without the fine print.

Creating unusual typographic effects

20. Because you can't crop type with an XPress text box, High developed his own workaround for the spine. He first drew a text box and, after entering his text, rotated it 90 degrees.

21. With the text box selected, he specified a background of None via the Text Box Specifications dialog (Modify command under the Item menu).

22. He then sent the text box behind the panels on each side by holding down the Option key and selecting the Send Backward command under the Item menu. This allowed him to move the text box one layer at a time. ☼: *Had he simply used the Send to Back command without the Option key, the black letters would have also gone behind the green background of the spine.*

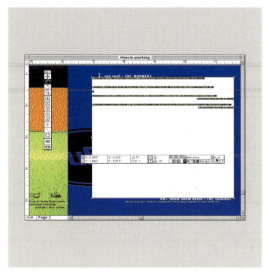

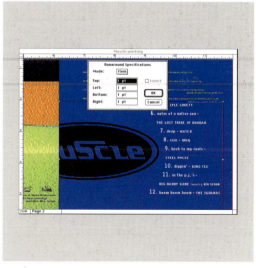

26. High then created an entirely new text box that contained the more detailed song information, set at 4 points (see Measurements palette).

Creating runarounds

27. The second group of text boxes listed the last half of the song titles, and wrapped around an invisible oval shape (which has been highlighted in the above screen). Notice also the highlighted number twelve, which High manually placed in his layout to override the specified text runaround.

28. High specified a one-point runaround on all sides of the oval picture box using the Runaround Specifications dialog under the Item menu (Command T).

Creating a Comp for a Package Design

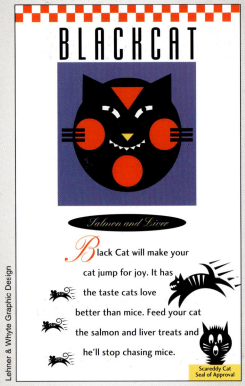

Designer Hugh Whyte created this color-ful package design for cat food using black-and-white clip art images colorized with XPress picture boxes. Shown here is the comp for the front panel of the box.

Lehner & Whyte Graphic Design

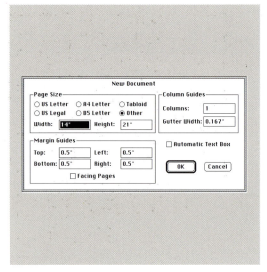

Setting up the page

1. Whyte's first step in composing the layout for the Black Cat cat food package was to create a Quark XPress page in the New Document dialog box (under the File menu) that was taller than the standard 8 1/2 by 11-inch page.

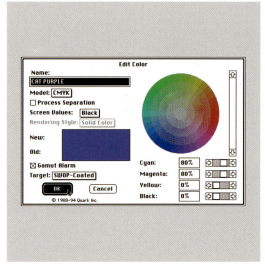

Laying the picture foundation

2. He then created a large picture box and filled it with a custom color, which he named "cat purple."

Colorizing the cat

6. Whyte assigned colors to the picture boxes via the Colors palette and used the Send to Back command (under the Item menu) to position all of the picture boxes behind the image of the cat.

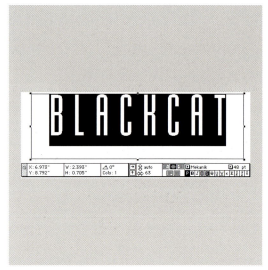

Specifying headline type

7. Whyte chose a strong geometric typeface for the headline, Mekanik set in 48 points, to match the bold lines and colors of his package design.

Creating the centerpiece for the design
3. Whyte chose a black-and-white clip art image of a cat (from the Fontek Attitudes collection, which he designed and illustrated for Letraset USA) as the centerpiece for his package design. 🎨 *The focal point of your layout doesn't need to be complex to be visually exciting.*

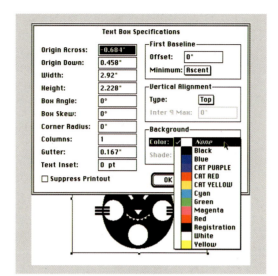

Layering text and picture boxes
4. The designer placed the cat inside a text box with a background of *None,* so that the purple background color of the picture box would show through the cutout areas of the cat image.

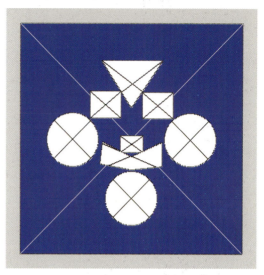

Adding accents
5. To add color accents to the cat's face, Whyte first drew picture boxes that approximated the shapes of the cat's facial features, using the polygon tool for the triangles, the circle tool for the cheeks and chin, and the square tool for the eyes and nose.

Specifying body type
8. A clean-looking, modern typeface called Charlotte Sans Medium set in 10 points with lots of leading (20 points) is the perfect complement to the accompanying text and graphics.

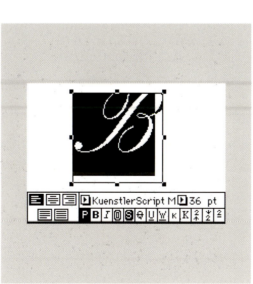

Typographic ornamentation
9. Whyte formatted the capital "B" in Kuenstler Medium, a delicate script face that adds counterpoint to the more geometric-looking design elements. 🎨 *Applying an initial cap is a wonderful way to add interest to body text in a wide variety of printed materials.*

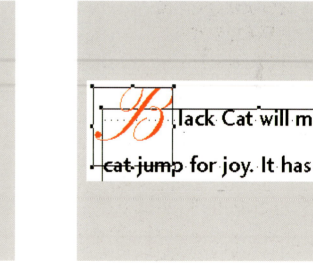

Creating an initial cap
10. Whyte drew a separate text box for the newly formatted "B," and instead of using an automatic runaround, manually positioned the initial cap within the main text.

Adding accent graphics

11. The designer used more clip art images from the same collection to add the whimsical touch of a cat chasing mice through the packaging's text. He rotated this image 10° from the Measurements palette.

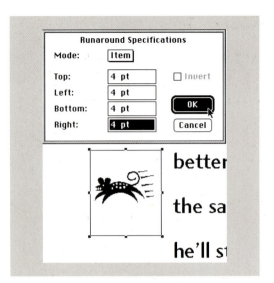

Creating an automatic runaround

12. To further the impression of the cat chasing the mice through the text, Whyte used the automatic runaround command on the middle mouse, specifying a 4-point runaround on all sides.

A final graphic element

13. Whyte then added one last graphic in the lower righthand corner in order to continue the whimsical theme of this package design. Another image from the Fontek DesignFonts collection embodies the scaredy cat idea.

Don't be a scaredy cat

14. Again using the Send to Back command, the designer created yellow picture boxes and sent them behind the image of the scaredy cat.

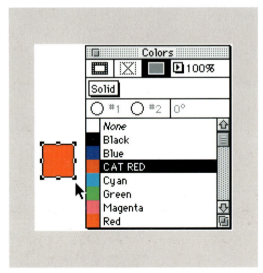

Adding the finishing touch

15. To create a border for the top of the package design, Whyte created a small text box with the picture box tool and colored it red via the Colors palette.

Better than copy and paste

16. He then used the Step and Repeat command under the Item menu to create two lines of red boxes across the top of the QuarkXPress document for a nice border effect.

Chapter Ten: Workgroup Publishing Tools

While desktop publishing technology has caused incredible advancement for publishers in the areas of pagination, typography, image editing, printing, and prepress techniques, it has also caused mass confusion in the area of workflow management. Once a delicate balance of skilled craftspeople with intertwined, yet clearly defined roles, the process of getting a publication out the door these days is made even more complicated with the use of personal computers. Although we can set type, lay out a page, and see proofs faster than we dared imagine a decade ago, the personal computer has served to isolate us from one another, diminishing our ability to keep track of revisions, manage the flow of documents from one person to another, and control who does what and when.

Fortunately, several software vendors have recognized this need and are developing programs that help publishers work together more cohesively and more efficiently. Better yet, many of these applications are designed to work directly with QuarkXPress. Among the many features of this complex genre of software, workgroup publishing programs offer revision tracking, version control, access privileges, scheduling, archiving, and planning modules. What was once the domain of a crusty old managing editor armed with a whiteboard can now be automated and monitored by the same crusty old managing editor using workgroup publishing software.

What's more, many of these tools allow several people to work on the same QuarkXPress document *at the same time*—a feat that became virtually impossible with the advent of personal computers and desktop publishing technology. Using today's workgroup publishing software, a designer can now lay out the page while a writer finishes the copy and an editor cuts the headline. In other words, we can regain some of the efficiency of the old publishing process without giving up the new technology.

That's not to say that all of our problems have been solved. While the software has improved greatly in the last year or two, today's workgroup publishing tools still need refinement. Nonetheless, it's important that we recognize this category of software as a critical piece of the publishing puzzle. I strongly believe that workflow management is one of the final frontiers in this age of "dtp," and that's why I've devoted a chapter to the topic in this book on page layout software.

In the following chapter, you'll find two examples of the many options available to desktop publishers today. The first example focuses on the Quark Publishing System (developed by Quark Inc.) and how it is used to manage the workflow at a daily newspaper. The second example highlights programs from North Atlantic Publishing Systems and shows how these products are used in a book publishing environment. There are dozens of other programs to keep your eye on if you're a QuarkXPress user, including the P.Ink Press System from Scitex Corp. and Ad Director and Page Director (featured at right) from Managing Editor Software.

It's an exciting time to be using electronic publishing technology, but remember: A publication that features beautiful design and brilliant copywriting won't do anyone any good if it never makes it to the printer. —*NJM*

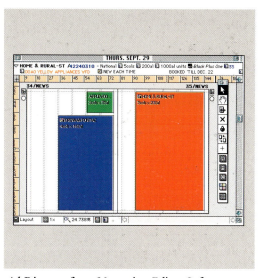

Ad Director from Managing Editor Software
1. One of the many tools that helps QuarkXPress users manage the publishing process is Ad Director ALS, an XTension that ties directly into XPress and automates advertising placement. Ad Director helps you keep track of ad and editorial ratios, color, coupons, and anything else related to advertising.

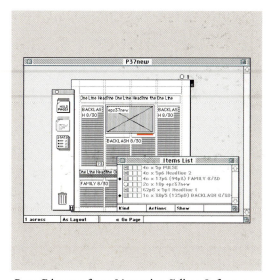

Page Director from Managing Editor Software
2. Another QuarkXPress XTension from Managing Editor Software, Page Director ELS helps you manage your entire publication, from organizing and gathering the elements of a story to arranging and rearranging pages.

Using the Quark Publishing System to Create a Newspaper

System Administrator Eric Jacobs takes us on a tour of The Daily Pennsylvanian's *workgroup publishing methods, using* QuarkXPress *and the* Quark Publishing System (QPS).

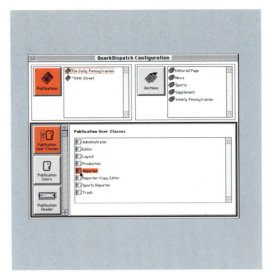

Setting up a publishing workflow

1. After QPS was installed at *The Daily Pennsylvanian*, Jacobs first defined the various sections of the publication using QPS' Dispatch FileManager. He also defined categories of user groups in the publishing environement, such as editorial and production.

Defining system privileges

2. As the QPS administrator, Jacobs then assigned privileges to user groups, determining what functions each user could perform on the system according to job description such as reporter, editor, layout, or production personnel.

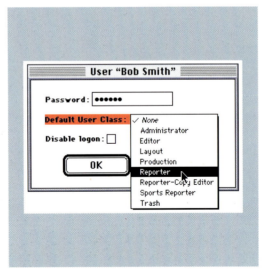

Assigning users to classes

6. To group *Daily Pennsylvanian* staff members according to job function, Jacobs used this pop-up dialog from the Publication User Classes button.

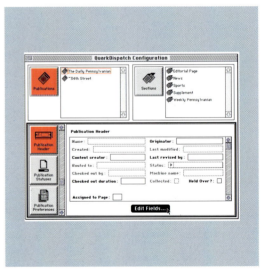

Creating publication header fields

7. QPS allows a system administrator to specify what type of information will be tracked by the Dispatch server, such as who originated (assigned) a document, who created the content, who revised it, and when.

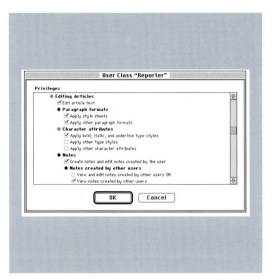

3. For example, reporters at *The Daily Pennsylvanian* are allowed to edit articles, apply style sheets, and create notes, but they cannot apply non-standard type styles to text or change layout attributes in a Quark XPress document.

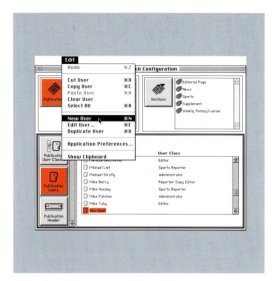

Creating new users

4. After Jacobs specified user groups, he then added individual users to QPS by selecting New User under the Edit menu in FileManager.

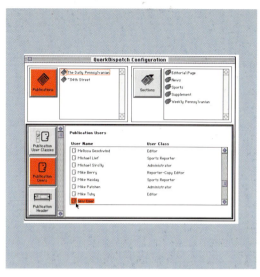

5. Here you can see the publication names (upper left of screen), the sections of a publication (upper right), and the publication's individual users and their User Class (bottom of screen).

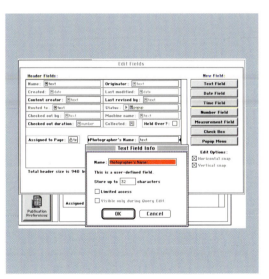

Creating custom header fields

8. Jacobs simply clicked on a New Field button to bring up all the header options for that particular field such as date, time, and number. Here he defined the information he wanted to appear in text fields.

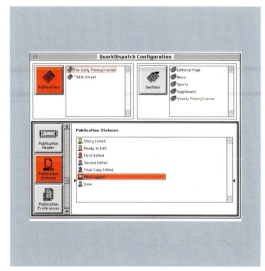

Specifying workflow statuses

9. How a document flows from one status to another is the heart of any workgroup publishing environment. QPS lets you reorder, add, and delete statuses.

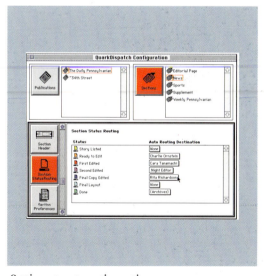

Setting up automatic routing

10. After determining the steps a document will travel through the publishing process (story listed, ready to edit, final copy edit, and so on), Jacobs set up automatic routing destinations for each completed step.

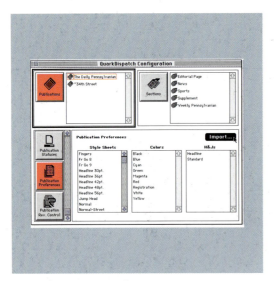

Importing XPress preferences

11. Another step in configuring QPS for *The Daily Pennsylvanian*'s needs was to import QuarkXPress preferences for style sheets, colors, hyphenation and justification, and the like.

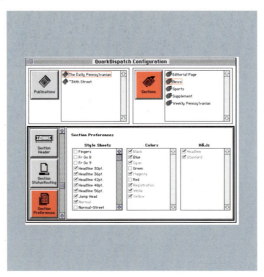

12. Once the XPress preferences have been imported, Jacobs specified which style attributes could be used in each section of the paper, such as News, Sports, and the Supplement.

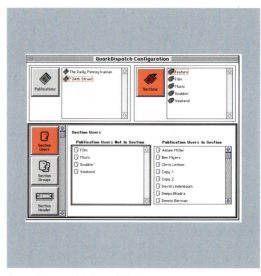

Handling multiple publications

13. In addition to its daily newspaper, *The Daily Pennsylvanian* also publishes a weekly arts and entertainment magazine, so Jacobs configured groups and users for that publication as well.

Logging on to the system

15. Now that the system was configured, users could log on to QPS by entering their name and password.

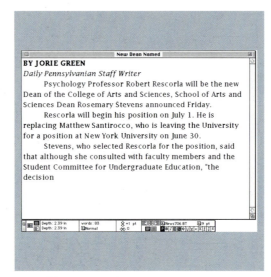

Launching CopyDesk

16. A writer that has logged on to the system will generally launch CopyDesk, QPS' word processing application.

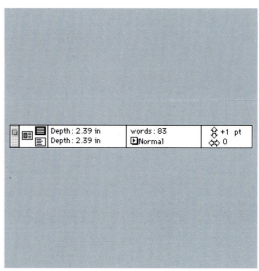

Monitoring article length

17. The CopyDesk Measurements palette reflects depth of the article in inches or picas, as well as word count and other text specifications.

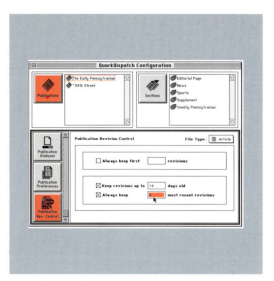

Tracking revisions

14. Jacobs also used the Dispatch FileManager to specify how long he wanted the system to track previous versions of documents and how many recent revisions should always be maintained by the system.

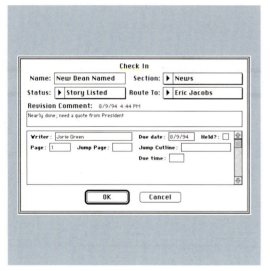

Checking in an article

18. After a reporter has written the first draft of an article, she checks it into QPS and routes it to the next person in the workflow.

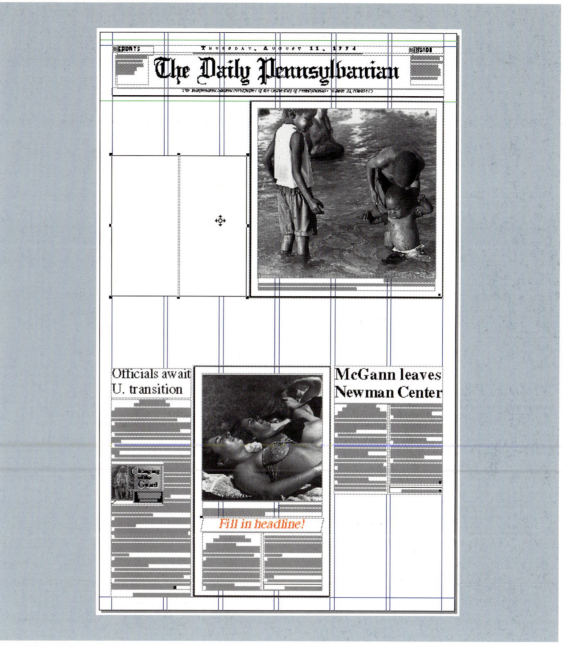

Parallel workflows

19. Meanwhile, a designer has begun to lay out the front page of the newspaper in QuarkXPress. Here we see the text box that has just been drawn for the lead story.

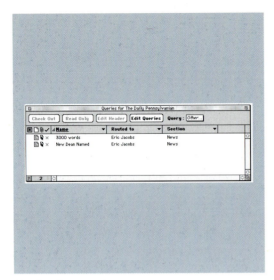

Performing searches

20. The QPS Query palette lets you search for articles and layouts based on name, who they have been routed to, section, and so on. A designer can use the query palette to search for a particular article that he is ready to lay out.

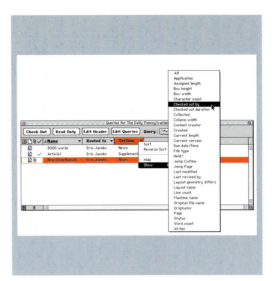

Customizing the query palette

21. New fields can be added to the Query palette via a pop-out menu, so that users can perform searches based on due date, status, column width, length, writer, page number, and so on.

Laying out stories with drag and drop

22. Once an article has been located via the Query palette, the designer simply drags the story icon from the palette to the appropriate text box on the Quark XPress layout.

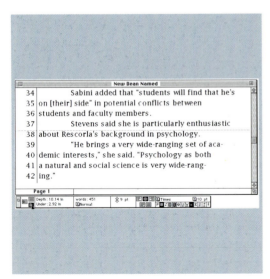

26. In Galley view, the writer or editor can see the text as it will be hyphenated and justified as determined by the actual page geometry of the Quark XPress layout in progress, but can still work in a point size and type style that is comfortable for long hours of writing and editing.

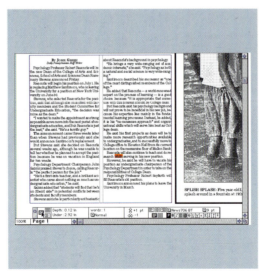

27. CopyDesk's WYSIWYG view lets writers and editors actually see the story as it will appear in the QuarkXPress layout, in the proper type style and point size, showing column widths and breaks. And although they can also see other elements of the page such as photographs, they can only work on the live text area surrounded by the blue border.

Changing page geometry

28. As a writer continues to work on the story in CopyDesk, the designer has added a photo to the QuarkXPress layout. The Dispatcher palette reflects this change in layout with a Geometry Differs status. The designer can then click the Update Geometry button so other users will be notified of the change.

23. When the mouse is released, the most current version of the story automatically flows into the designated text box. Along with the Query palette, you can also see the Dispatcher palette open, which is tracking the items placed in the QuarkXPress layout.

Checking out an existing article

24. If another writer or editor wants to work on a story that's already been written and checked into the system, the selected story can be "checked out" via the Query palette. This way, no two people can be making changes to the same story at the same time.

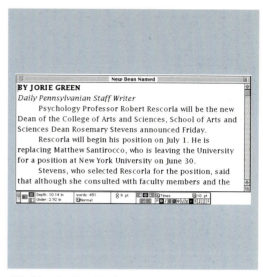

Working in CopyDesk

25. A writer or editor working in CopyDesk can view text in three views. The first view is Full-Screen view, which is similar to any other word processing program, in which a writer composes text in any type size and style across the entire screen.

Updating page geometry

29. A notice then appears at the writer's workstation that the layout has been changed, and asks whether or not the file should be updated to reflect the latest change. If the writer chooses not to view the change, the file will be updated when the story is checked in.

30. The writer has chosen to update the page geometry and now has a current view of the QuarkXPress layout with the new photo that has been added by the designer.

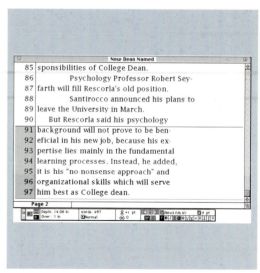

Updating in Galley view

31. Since the photo was added to the layout, the story has now become too long for the allotted space. The writer returns to CopyDesk's Galley view, which indicates overflowed text with a gray bar.

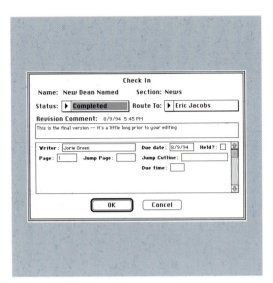

Checking in a final version

32. The writer has adjusted the length of the copy and is now ready to check the article back into the system, typing a note to the next user in the Revision Comment field.

Assigning a headline

33. Moving back to the layout station, the designer is now ready to assign a headline to a writer based on type size and available space. After drawing a text box, he clicks on the Assign button in the Dispatcher palette.

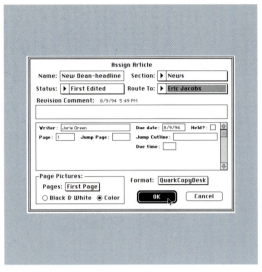

34. This brings up the Assign Article dialog box, in which the designer can route the assignment to a particular person, indicate a due date and time, and type comments.

Updating text

37. Back at the layout station, the designer receives a notice that the "Text Differs." He simply clicks the Update Content button…

38. …and the new headline appears in the appropriate text box.

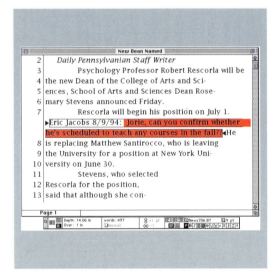

Inserting notes

39. When working in CopyDesk's Full-Screen and Galley views, users can insert inline notes without affecting the line count of the story. The name of the note's creator and the date the note was written is automatically entered at the beginning of the note.

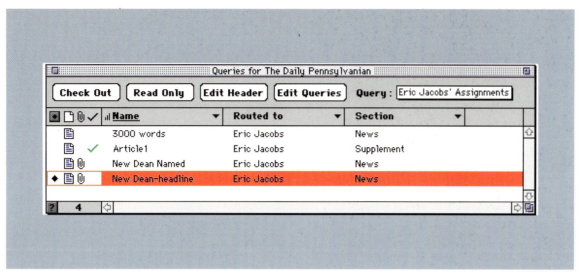

Receiving an assignment

35. Once the designer has sent the headline assignment to the Dispatch server, a notice then shows up on the assignee's Query palette along with an audio sound signifying that a new assignment has come in. Here you can see the new assignment highlighted in red with a diamond marker on the left of the palette.

Fulfilling an assignment

36. The editor then launches CopyDesk in WYSIWYG mode to write the headline directly into the QuarkXPress layout.

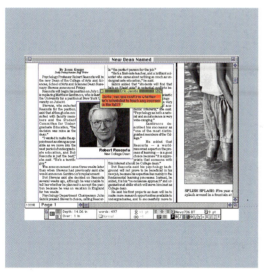

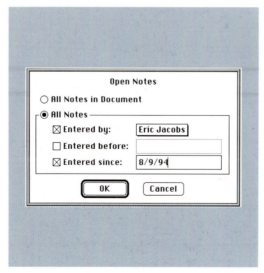

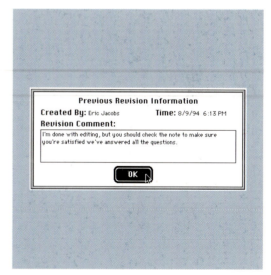

40. The same note appears as a Post-It-like note in CopyDesk's WYSIWYG view. The user can specify whether to close notes or open notes.

Viewing notes

41. Users can also set criteria for which notes they wish to view according to creator and date.

Viewing revision comments

42. When CopyDesk and QuarkXPress users check out an article that has been revised, they will see any Revision Comments attached to that version of the article.

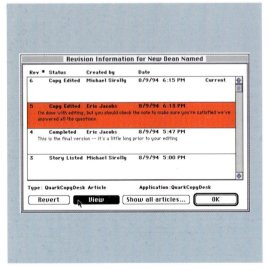

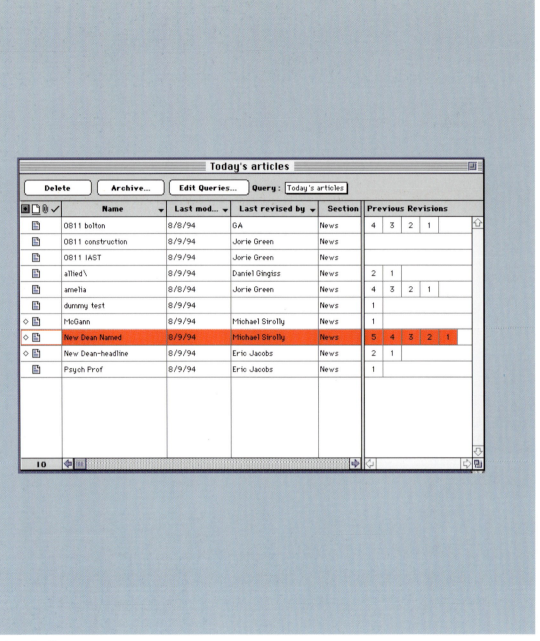

Viewing several revisions

43. QPS users can review all saved revisions for a particular article by choosing View Revisions from the QuarkDispatch menu.

44. QPS' View Revisions command lets users view summary information about each revision, the date and time it was created, the status of the article, and so on.

The Dispatch FileManager

45. QPS' FileManager application shows users a revision history for each article within a publication or section. Authorized users can open and delete individual revisions from the FileManager.

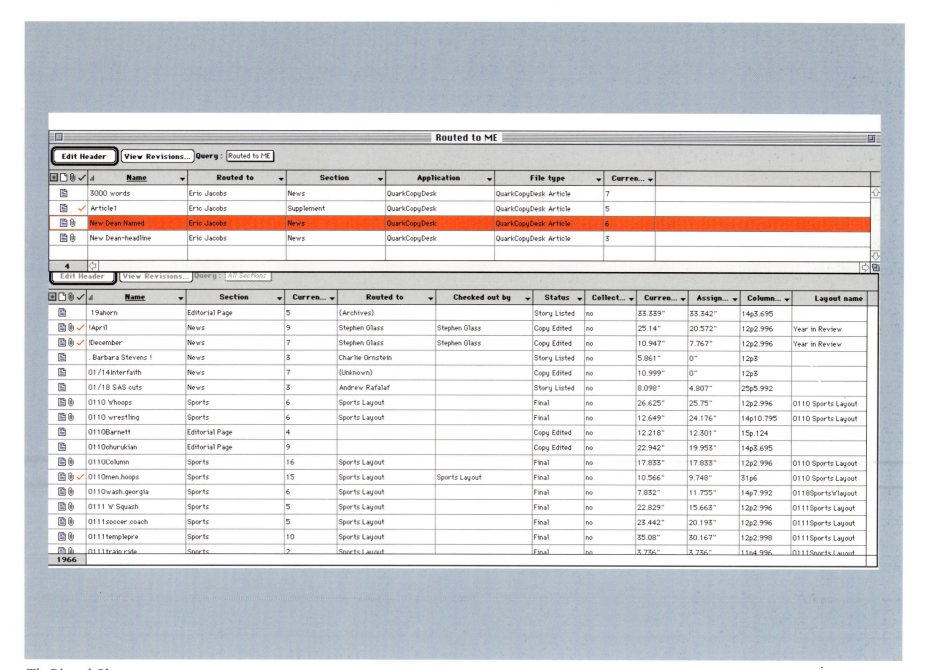

Routed to ME

	Name	Routed to	Section	Application	File type	Curren...	
📄	3000 words	Eric Jacobs	News	QuarkCopyDesk	QuarkCopyDesk Article	7	
📄 ✓	Article1	Eric Jacobs	Supplement	QuarkCopyDesk	QuarkCopyDesk Article	5	
📄 📎	New Dean Named	Eric Jacobs	News	QuarkCopyDesk	QuarkCopyDesk Article	6	
📄 📎	New Dean-headline	Eric Jacobs	News	QuarkCopyDesk	QuarkCopyDesk Article	3	

4

Edit Header | View Revisions... | Query : All Sections

	Name	Section	Curren...	Routed to	Checked out by	Status	Collect...	Curren...	Assign...	Column...	Layout name
📄	19ahorn	Editorial Page	5	{Archives}		Story Listed	no	33.339"	33.342"	14p3.695	
📄📎✓	!April	News	9	Stephen Glass	Stephen Glass	Copy Edited	no	25.14"	20.572"	12p2.996	Year in Review
📄📎✓	!December	News	7	Stephen Glass	Stephen Glass	Copy Edited	no	10.947"	7.767"	12p2.996	Year in Review
📄	. Barbara Stevens !	News	3	Charlie Ornstein		Story Listed	no	5.861"	0"	12p3	
📄	01/14Interfaith	News	7	{Unknown}		Copy Edited	no	10.999"	0"	12p3	
📄	01/18 SAS cuts	News	3	Andrew Rafalaf		Story Listed	no	8.098"	4.807"	25p5.992	
📄📎	0110 Whoops	Sports	6	Sports Layout		Final	no	26.625"	25.75"	12p2.996	0110 Sports Layout
📄📎	0110 wrestling	Sports	6	Sports Layout		Final	no	12.649"	24.176"	14p10.795	0110 Sports Layout
📄	0110Barnett	Editorial Page	4			Copy Edited	no	12.218"	12.301"	15p.124	
📄	0110churukian	Editorial Page	9			Copy Edited	no	22.942"	19.953"	14p3.695	
📄📎	0110Column	Sports	16	Sports Layout		Final	no	17.833"	17.833"	12p2.996	0110 Sports Layout
📄📎✓	0110men.hoops	Sports	15	Sports Layout	Sports Layout	Final	no	10.566"	9.748"	31p6	0110 Sports Layout
📄📎	0110wash.georgia	Sports	6	Sports Layout		Final	no	7.832"	11.755"	14p7.992	0118SportsWlayout
📄📎	0111 W Squash	Sports	5	Sports Layout		Final	no	22.829"	15.663"	12p2.996	0111Sports Layout
📄📎	0111soccer.coach	Sports	5	Sports Layout		Final	no	23.442"	20.193"	12p2.996	0111Sports Layout
📄📎	0111templepre	Sports	10	Sports Layout		Final	no	35.08"	30.167"	12p2.998	0111Sports Layout
📄📎	0111train ride	Sports	2	Sports Layout		Final	no	3.736"	3.736"	11p4.996	0111Sports Layout

1966

The Dispatch Planner

46. In addition to configuring and tracking workflows, QPS lets users assign articles and monitor their status through the Dispatch Planner application. Above you can see two tiled windows in which the managing editor can view all the articles related to the publication, whether or not they are checked out, their current length and assigned length, on what page they appear, and so forth. The managing editor can make additional assignments from the Planner.

Using NAPS Technology
in
Book Production

St. Remy Press

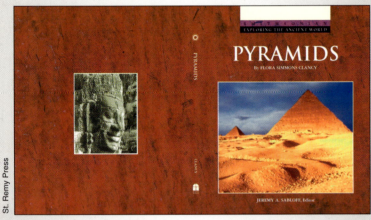

The North Atlantic Publishing Systems' (NAPS) suite of products helps publishers manage the flow of documents through a workgroup publishing environment. Edward Renaud, an electronic publishing consultant for Graphor Consultation, shows us how St. Remy Press in Montreal uses NAPS and QuarkXPress to produce a wide variety of high-quality books, including this four-color book called Pyramids for the Smithsonian Institution.

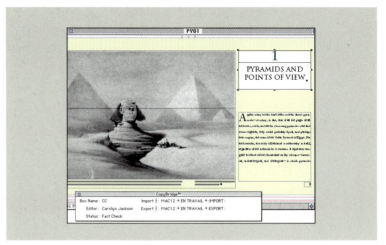

Setting the stage
1. Here is an example of what the opening spread of *Pyramids* looks like on-screen. Much of the work that St. Remy Press produces is graphic-intensive, with a large number of text boxes containing captions.

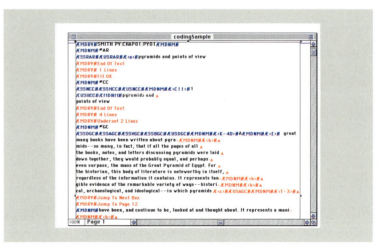

Viewing copyfit information
4. If a text file needs to be exported back out of the XPress document for editorial adjustment, CopyBridge maintains the copyfit information from the XPress layout (such as line breaks) in the XyWrite text file (above). In addition to line breaks, an editor can also see column breaks, page jumps, and underset or overset amounts.

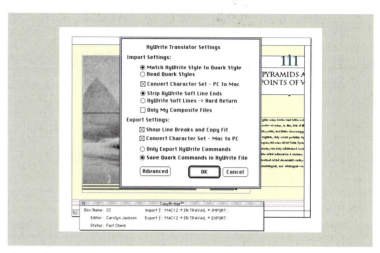

Using CopyBridge to import text

2. One of the first NAPS products that St. Remy Press installed was Copy-Bridge, a QuarkXPress XTension that allows text created in a program like XyWrite to be automatically imported to and exported from XPress. A designer assigns a name to a particular text box (above), which in effect creates a link between the text box on the XPress layout and the appropriate XyWrite text file. A single XyWrite file can contain the text for many XPress text boxes. After the captions within each XyWrite file have been tagged, CopyBridge automatically flows them into the correct text boxes.

Importing XPress tags

3. A designer can also use CopyBridge to import XyWrite's formatting codes as XPress style tags.

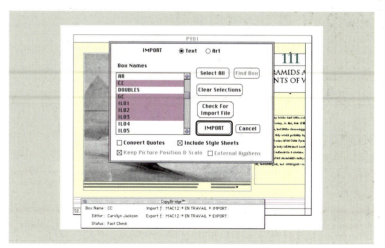

Making use of CopyBridge's "Hot Import" mode

5. Users can activate CopyBridge's Hot Import mode by specifying a Hot Import folder and a Master Export folder, as shown above. This means that the CopyBridge XTension at the QuarkXPress layout station will continually monitor the Hot Import folder until it finds that a XyWrite file has been placed there. CopyBridge reads the XPress file name in the XyWrite file, opens the file, and automatically exports the text into the XPress layout. If more than one XyWrite file has been placed in the Hot Import folder, Copy-Bridge will automatically perform a batch import.

Viewing a batch import

6. Here you can see the batch import dialog box with preferences to convert quotes and include style sheets. CopyBridge can also perform batch imports on art files, with the option to maintain the picture's position and scale.

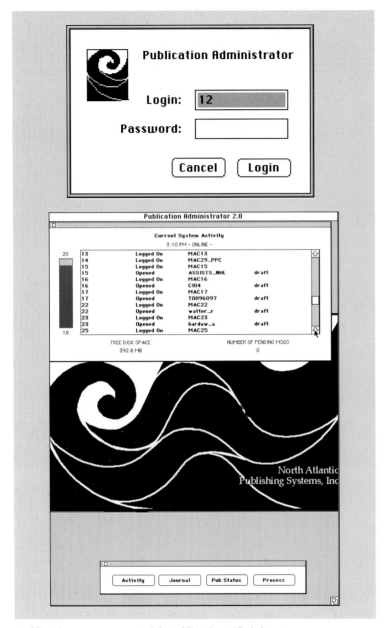

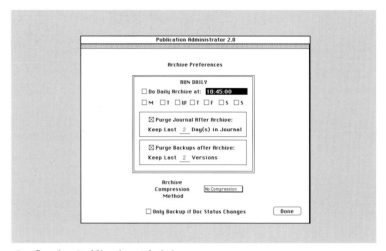

Configuring Publication Administrator

8. Renaud configured the PA server at St. Remy Press to run a daily backup at 6:45 p.m., and to keep the last two versions of backups and journals. Other configuration options include interface preferences, the ability to enable Apple Events, and XTension preferences.

Seamless version control

11. PA users at St. Remy Press can select either a project, a chapter, or an XPress document to work on. If the requested file is currently in use, the server will not allow another user to open that file. If the requested file is available, PA first automatically copies the file onto the user's hard drive, then renames the file on the server with a version number. When the user is finished working on a file and closes it, PA again automatically copies the updated file onto the server, then renames the user's local file as a backup copy. Above is an example of all the tracking information that PA maintains for a document.

Publication management with Publication Administrator

7. The next major product in the North Atlantic line of software is Publication Administrator, which helps users track and manage XPress documents. Based on a Fourth Dimension database, the Publication Administrator (PA) server maintains a list of projects and keeps track of each XPress file as it is being worked on by a variety of users. To work on a file, a user first logs onto the PA system (top). Managers can also view a report of all the activity on the PA server (bottom).

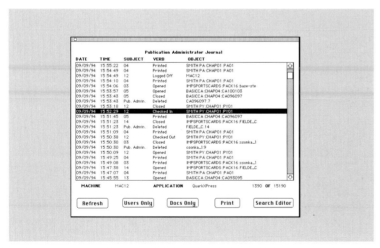

Setting up user classes

9. Publication Administrator also enabled Renaud to configure user classes and privileges for all the users on the system at St. Remy Press. For example, users are categorized according to job function such as designers, writers, and editors. Renaud used the above dialog box to specify which XPress menus, North Atlantic menus, and XTension menus designers could access when logged on to Publication Administrator.

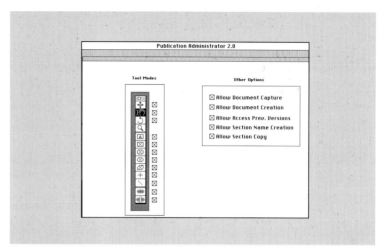

Accessing tools

10. He could even define which tools in the QuarkXPress tool palette a user could enable using the above dialog box.

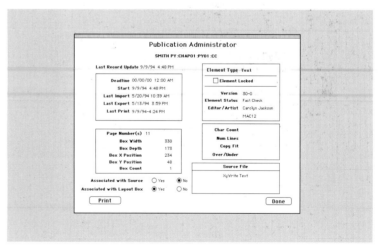

Keeping a journal

12. Every time someone at St. Remy press opens, closes, or prints a file, PA records that activity in a journal (above).

Tracking individual boxes

13. And because each text box has been named with CopyBridge, PA can track the activity for an individual text or picture box. The above dialog box tells a manager which person is responsible for a particular box, whether or not there is something in the assigned box, and if so, what the character count is and whether or not the text is overset or underset.

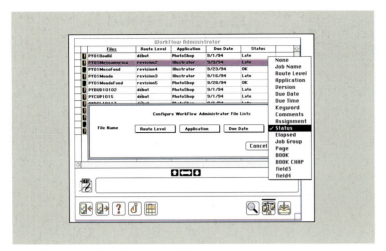

Tracking more than just XPress documents

14. Because St. Remy Press works with more than text files and XPress documents (as do most other publishers), the users there needed a means of tracking art files being created and edited in programs like Adobe Photoshop and Adobe Illustrator. That's where Workflow Administrator (WA) enters the picture. WA can track files created in *any* Macintosh application. Here you can see WA's pop-up menu for configuring database fields such as job name, due date, status, and type of application.

Checking out a file

15. As with PA, users check files in and out of the system so that no two users can make changes to a document at the same time. The WA file server (above) looks similar to a spreadsheet. The highlighted file with the checkmark next to it has been checked out. St. Remy uses a lot of freelance editors and illustrators, who check documents in and out of the WA server from remote locations in the same fashion as St. Remy's on-site employees.

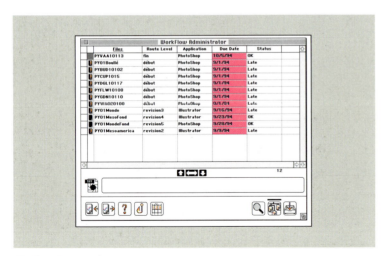

Performing queries

18. Users can perform queries on the WA database according to status, file name, application, route level, due date (above), or any number of conditions.

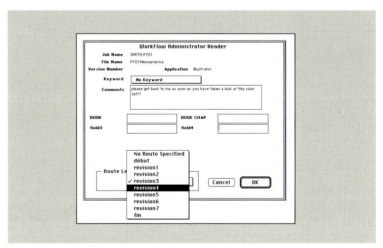

Establishing routing levels

19. An important step in any publication management system is to establish the flow of documents from one person to the next, or routing levels. Renaud set up routing levels according to the type of project. For example, files at St. Remy travel along three basic routes: one for editorial, one for art (above), and another for scanned images.

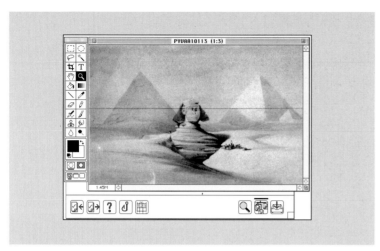

Tracking a variety of applications

16. The beauty of WA is its ability to integrate any application into its seamless version control procedure. Here is a Photoshop document for the *Pyramids* book that has been opened by an artist at St. Remy. The artist simply logged onto WA and selected the above file. WA automatically copied the file onto the artist's hard drive, renamed the file left on the server, automatically launched Photoshop, and opened the local copy of the file.

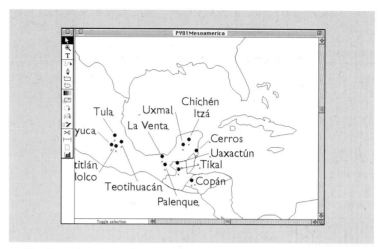

17. Here's another piece of art for the *Pyramids* book that was created in Adobe Illustrator and automatically opened by the WA server for another artist.

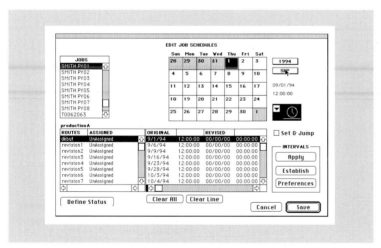

Creating schedules

20. A killer-feature of the NAPS workgroup publishing software is WA's scheduling module, which lets managers establish due dates for every intermediate step based on a target due date for the entire publication.

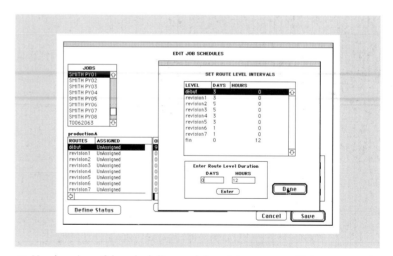

21. Here's a view of the scheduling module as it lets you specify how many days and hours each user class should spend on a particular level of a project.

Using XTensions to Enhance QuarkXPress

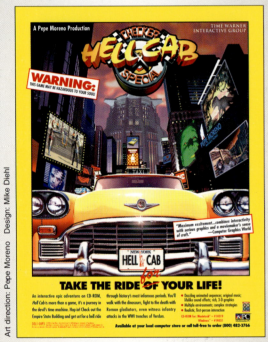

QuarkXPress XTensions are software programs developed by independent programmers that let users customize and enhance the capabilities of XPress. Using artwork for an ad designed by Mike Diehl, we'll show you just a few of the hundreds of XTensions available today. For information on where to purchase the Xtensions featured in this book, see the list of vendors on page 138.

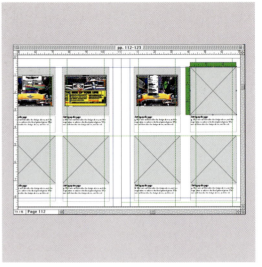

BeyondMeasure from Acrobyte

1. This nifty little XTension is the first offering from a new company called Acrobyte, founded by former Quark programmers. BeyondMeasure expands the capabilities of XPress rulers by providing two floating rulers. Above is the Beyond Measure Preferences dialog, in which you can specify the color of the rulers.

2. When you press Command Shift and click on either ruler, both of the rulers (one horizontal and one vertical) will snap to the currently selected item. Command-click will cause just the ruler you clicked on to snap to the selected item. If nothing is selected, the ruler(s) will snap to the edges of your document.

6. In addition to the ability to pull guides from the floating rulers, BeyondMeasure also offers a measure tool, found in the XPress Tool palette when the XTension is loaded. The measure tool lets you measure the distance between any two points in a document, including diagonals. After clicking the measure tool, click once on your starting point (above)…

7. …then drag the crosshairs to your second endpoint. You'll be able to see not only the width and height dimensions, but the total distance and angle between your two endpoints.

3. One of the most useful features of BeyondMeasure is the ability to measure *between* items—a difficult, if not impossible, task in XPress. Here you can see the horizontal ruler, which can be dragged with the grabber hand tool, as it is used to measure the distance between two picture boxes on this layout.

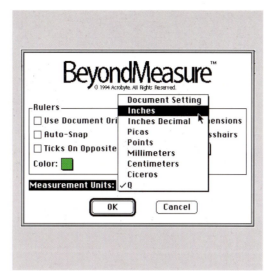

4. Using the BeyondMeasure Preferences dialog, you can specify the measurement units of your floating rulers in inches, inches decimal, picas, points, millimeters, centimeters, ciceros, Q (Japanese typesetting units), or to match the settings of your document.

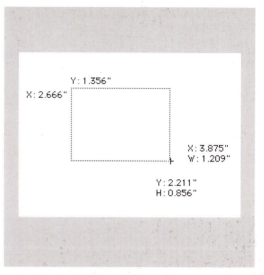

5. Another handy feature of BeyondMeasure is the ability to view "Instant Dimensions" as you draw a text box, picture box, or line on-screen. While some of these measurements are available in the XPress Measurements palette, it's nice to view the dimensions right next to the item as it's being drawn.

Azalea UPC-EAN XTension

8. This wonderful program from Azalea Software makes creating bar codes a breeze. After you've installed the OCR fonts and have loaded the XTension into your XTensions folder, simply select the Azalea XTension from the Utilities menu.

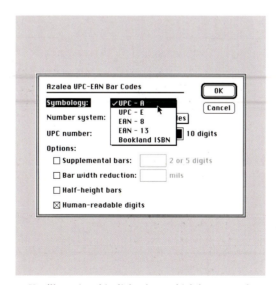

9. You'll receive this dialog box, which lets you select which type of bar code you want to create (UPC A and E, used in the U.S., EAN 8 and 13, used in Europe, or Bookland, used for ISBN numbers). As of this writing, the next version of the Azalea UPC-EAN XTension will also include the ability to create JAN bar codes, used in Japan.

10. After typing in the numbers for your bar code, the Azalea XTension automatically creates an EPS graphic and places it directly into your XPress document. The symbols can be scaled proportionally or truncated in half horizontally for smaller items such as labels.

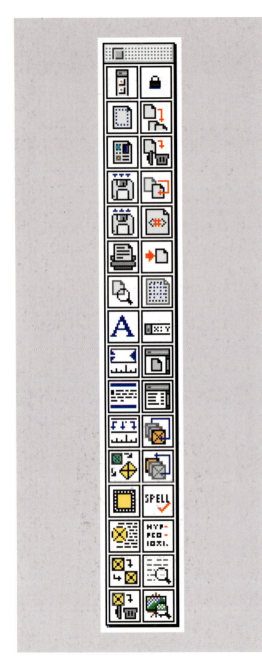

Kitchen Sink, a lowly apprentice production

11. This handy XTension from a lowly apprentice production (alap) claims to do everything but the dishes. Kitchen Sink's Command Pad (shown above), provides one-click access to nearly every XPress menu item, plus a few more.

12. For example, simply clicking the Get Picture icon on the Command Pad when a picture box is selected will give you the Get Picture dialog, without having to go through the File menu or remember any keyboard shortcuts. Another click on the Command Pad opens a document, saves the page as an EPS file, hides the Measurements palette, and so on.

ScaleIt, alap

17. This XTension lets users scale lines, text and picture boxes, and their contents—individually or as a group. While you can scale items in XPress, ScaleIt provides an entire range of options (above) that make complex scaling operations quicker and easier.

13. Another feature of the Kitchen Sink XTension is the Co-Pilot, a palette that displays a proxy of the current page or spread. By simply clicking on any point in the proxy, Co-Pilot provides instant scrolling to that point. It even leaves a red flag in the proxy to show the last place you clicked.

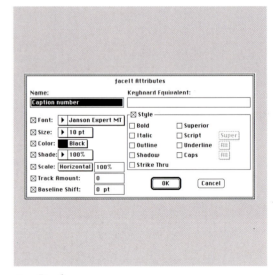

ƒaceIt, alap

18. ƒaceIt provides character-level text styling, a frequently requested feature for XPress. ƒaceIt also includes the ƒaceIt palette, which operates in much the same way as the XPress Style palette, but lets you apply character-based styles with a single click.

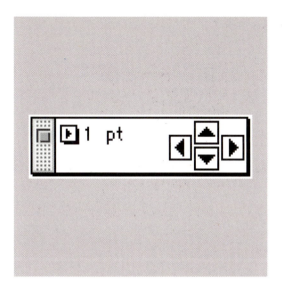

14. Also included with the Kitchen Sink XTension is NudgeIt, a palette that lets you nudge selected items, an image within a picture box, or the text-insertion cursor within a text box. Specify your nudge increments via the pop-up menu, enter a new value in the number field, or Option-click the arrow buttons to move items one-tenth of the nudge amount.

15. The Scale/Shift palette (also incuded in Kitchen Sink) lets you scale text horizontally and vertically—plus perform baseline shift operations—without having to go through dialog boxes. Above you can see the Scale/Shift palette being used to apply a negative baseline shift to every other letter in the headline.

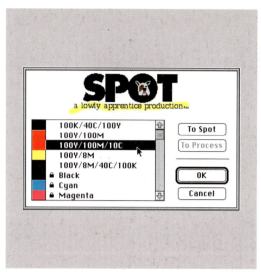

16. Yet another feature of this XTension (it really does include everything but the kitchen sink) is the Spot dialog box, which lets you convert spot colors to process and vice versa. You can even hear Spot bark if you click the right place in the dialog box.

Layer Manager, alap

19. Working with all the different layers of items in a complex XPress document can get confusing. Layer Manager II lets users group items together according to which layer of the document they belong. You can even lock certain layers or make them invisible.

WhatzIt, alap

20. This way-cool XTension provides all sorts of information on images placed in your XPress document. Just click on the gold triangle in the upper left corner of the picture box, and you'll receive this pop-up dialog box, which gives you the graphic's file type, resolution, color, path, embedded fonts, and so on.

Crop & RegIt, alap

21. Crop & RegIt lets you automatically place crop marks, registration marks, a CMYK tag, color bars, and grayscale bars on any selected element of an XPress page.

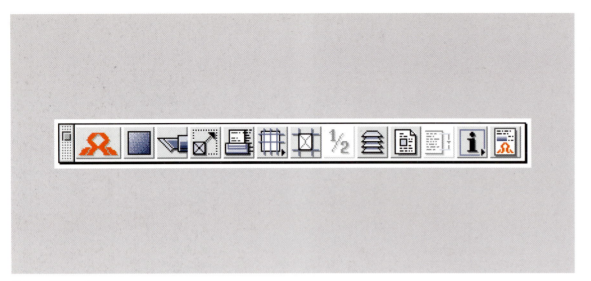

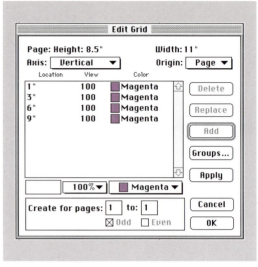

Scitex XTensions

22. The Scitex XTensions from Scitex Corporation include twelve sets of XTensions for designers and production artists using QuarkXPress. The Launchpad, above, is a floating palette that provides access to any Scitex XTensions installed on your system. The button on the left of the Launchpad (with the Scitex logo) offers online help for each XTension, including step-by-step instructions and tips.

Scitex Grids & Guides

23. Many of the best designs in this book are based on a grid system. The Scitex Grids & Guides XTension lets you build complex grids that can be saved and imported from one XPress document to another.

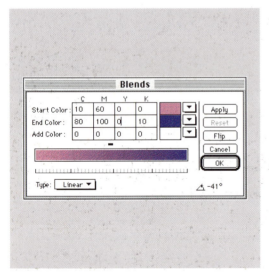

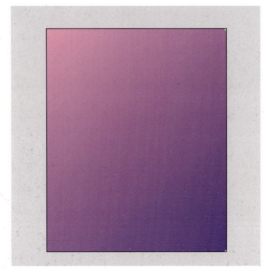

Scitex Image Tools

27. This group of XTensions includes the Scitex Blends XTension, which provides even more options for creating blends than Quark's own Cool Blends XTension.

28. Here's a two-color linear blend we created from the Blends dialog box. This XTension lets you create blends of up to 14 colors, control the blend rate between two colors, and specify blends on a path of any angle.

29. Another XTension included in the Scitex Image Tools set is Scitex Silhouettes, which lets you silhouette a picture, masking out the surrounding area for text wraps, outlines, shadows, and other special effects. Above you can see the Silhouette button on the Launchpad activated as we began creating a silhouette of the taxi.

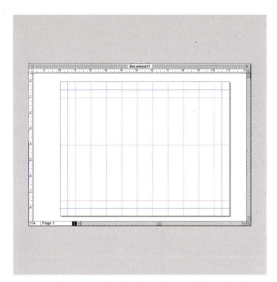

24. Here's a somewhat basic grid we whipped up in just a few minutes using the Edit Grid dialog box. Another nice feature of this XTension is the ability to place guides along the sides of a picture box using the Guides To Item button on the Launchpad.

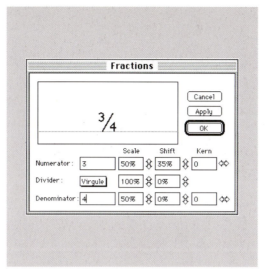

Scitex Fractions

25. This Xtension lets you fine tune the appearance of fractions, with endless possibilities for kerning, shifting, and scaling each component of the fraction, including the divider mark.

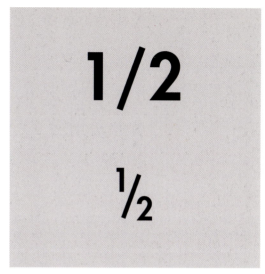

26. Here's an example of how the Fractions XTension helps improve the appearance of a fraction. The top example shows the fraction as it would normally appear when typed in an XPress text box, and the bottom example shows the same fraction with the XTension's Virgule option and kerning applied.

30. Here's the result of our silhouette, which we created by clicking along the outline of the taxi with the Silhouette cursor.

31. As you can see, we had loads of fun with this XTension, and copied our silhouette from the original XPress document onto the pages of this book. We then resized it by pressing Command Option Shift while we dragged the picture box handles, but first we had to disable the Kitchen Sink XTension from alap, which uses the same keyboard shortcut for its Co-Pilot. ☀: *Installing too many XTensions onto your system can cause a variety of incompatibilities; it's best to install one XTension at a time and work with it for a day or two before installing another.*

BureauManager from CompuSense

32. If you like XPress' Collect for Output feature, you'll love BureauManager. This XTension helps you prepare QuarkXPress files for the service bureau by extracting information regarding which fonts and graphics are required to print the document.

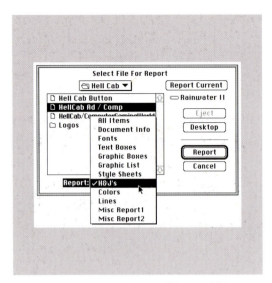

33. You can generate reports on all items within a document, or on specific aspects such as style sheets or colors. BureauManager's Updater Defaults feature will automatically update missing graphics, while the FontMover feature lets you collect and move a file's screen and printer fonts, including those embedded in EPS graphics.

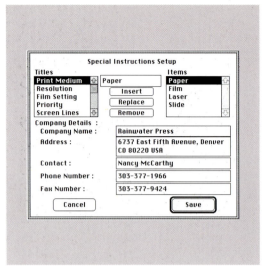

34. BureauManager's Special Instructions dialog box lets you specify print media, resolution, film settings, shipping instructions, and contact information for your service bureau.

Vision Contents from Vision's Edge

38. It would be ideal if XPress included table of contents and index generation capabilities within the main application, but because it doesn't, you can make do with XTensions such as this one, which creates a table of contents based on style sheet usage.

Picture Dæmon from Vision's Edge

39. Picture Dæmon lets you search for graphics based on file type, name, or even date. It can also provide path information, modification date, and file size for a selected graphic, automatically update a picture, and print out a document's entire picture list.

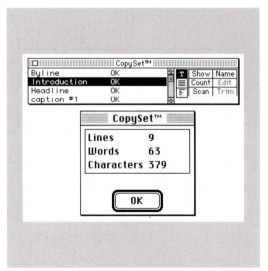

CopySet from Vision's Edge

40. This editorial utility's primary function is to show overset and underset information for a given text box, but we find its ability to provide line, word, and character counts useful (especially if you're crazy enough to use QuarkXPress as a word processor).

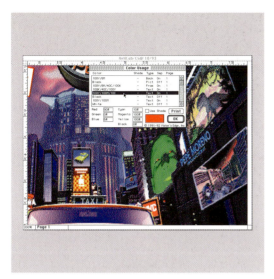

Color Usage from Vision's Edge

35. Vision's Edge is one of the more prolific XTension developers, as you can see by the sampling of Vision's Edge XTensions on this page. Color Usage is a neat program that lists the colors of a document, their RGB or CMYK values, as well as whether or not the process separation button has been checked.

ColorChange from Vision's Edge

36. Using an XPress-like Find/Change interface, Color Change lets you selectively search and replace colors and shades based on text boxes, pictures boxes, background colors, and frames within an XPress document.

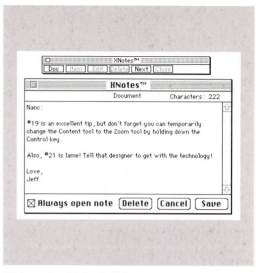

XNotes by Vision's Edge

37. We love this XTension, which gives you the ability to embed Post-It-like notes in an XPress document. The user has the option to view the notes or hide them, and they can also be printed in a report format. XNotes comes with a read-only version of the program, so other XPress users can view your notes.

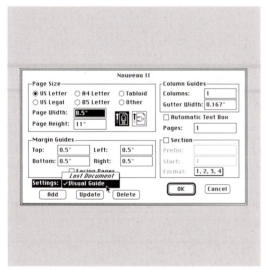

Nouveau II from Vision's Edge

41. This simple XTension gives you the ability to save multiple new document settings (such as paper width and height, margins, and columns) so that you don't have to repeatedly input your frequently used settings when creating a new XPress document.

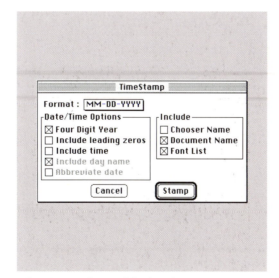

TimeStamp from Vision's Edge

42. Automatically updated each time a document is saved, TimeStamp helps XPress users keep track of revisions. We also like Vision's Edge JobSlug XTension, which can record a document's user name, job number, editor, client, document name, and time it was saved and printed.

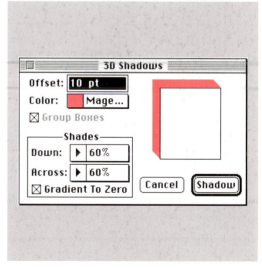

ShadowMaster from Vision's Edge

43. Drop shadows tend to be amateurish, but this little utility lets you automatically create fun shadow effects directly in XPress—even shadows with gradient blends.

11

Using Xdata to Format an Annual Report

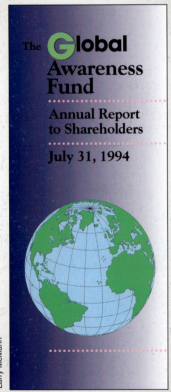

Larry McMunn of McMunn Associates in Collingswood, NJ shows us how his firm uses Em Software's Xdata XTension and QuarkXPress to turn raw financial data into a well-designed annual report.

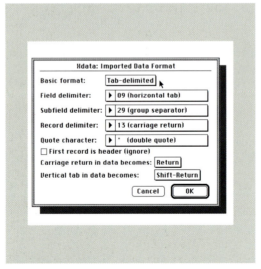

```
010004004950006203.00.0000000070960.5800072768.750000064000004HONG0KONG0SHANGHAI0BANKING00000000000
010045751000028233.00.0000000075377.7900085619.750000064000004INDIA0FUND0B00000000000000000000000*¬
010005341011963750.00.000000004362596.1604296856.820000064000004LONRHO0PLC0000000000000000000000000*-
010007192101325797.36.0000000003482385.3004264921.080000064000004VODAFONE0GROUP0PLC¢¢¢¢¢¢¢¢¢¢¢¢¢¢
010071825210073050.00.000000004285480.9504821300.000000064000008PHILIPPINE0LONG0DISTANCE0TELEPHONE¢
010060895081059400.00.00000002893030.5203904722.410000064000009BANK0INTERNATIONAL0INDONESIA0(FOREI
010062894490823500.00.00000003249453.7701422771.250000064000009DUTA0ANGGADA0REALTY0(FOREIGN)0000000
010064677062029500.00.00000003050786.8103132377.330000064000009PT0JAPFA0SHARES0(FOREIGN)¢¢¢¢¢¢¢¢¢
010064806730303000.00.00000001690920.1301256392.530000064000009KABEL0INDO0(FOREIGN)¢¢¢¢¢¢¢¢¢¢¢¢¢¢¢
010063666760591000.00.00000004192695.5005543873.360000064000010GENTING0BERHAD¢¢¢¢¢¢¢¢¢¢¢¢¢¢¢¢¢¢¢
010064859570137600.00.0000000020829.0400250621.840000064000010KELANAMAS0INDUSTRIES0BERHAD0WARRANTS
010065563250816000.00.00000004129955.5605230564.780000064000010MALAYAN0BANKING0BERHAD¢¢¢¢¢¢¢¢¢¢¢
010065568751593320.00.00000003312622.3303923359.780000064000010MALAYSIAN0HELICOPTER0SERVICES0BERHA
010067544531538300.00.00000005163903.3306433382.840000064000010TECHNOLOGY0RESOURCES0INDUSTRIES0BEH
010068289490059500.0000.0000000161864.1400150000.000000064000010SOUTHERN0BANK0BERHAD¢¢¢¢¢¢¢¢¢¢¢
010068607148402000.0000.0000002677531.9402233089.700000064000010KELANAMAS0INDUSTRIES0BERHAD¢¢¢¢¢
010067951284280000.0000.0000003508121.5203431032.190000064000011SEMBAWANG0CORP.0LIMITED0ORDINARY0SH
010069167702394000.0000.0000001766029.5902363230.420000064000011UNITED0OVERSEAS0BANK¢¢¢¢¢¢¢¢¢¢¢
010060081381027000.0000.0000003585422.7704396714.850000064000012ADVANCED0INFORMATION0SERVICES0LIMIT
010060745715904000.0000.0000003038099.0801991710.840000064000012BANGKOK0LAND0PUBLIC0COMPANY0LIMITED
```

Preparing raw data

1. When used in conjunction with QuarkXPress, you can use Xdata to automatically format data exported from Mac or PC databases and spreadsheets and even mainframe systems. Xdata can also be used to automatically import graphics (in any format supported by XPress) for catalogs and directories. Above you can see raw financial data as it was exported from the mainframe of a specialized mutual funds manager before it has been cleaned up by McMunn Associates and formatted by Xdata.

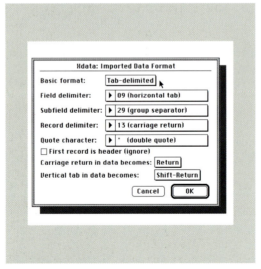

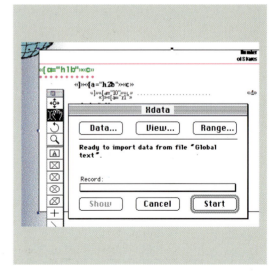

Importing the data

5. Once the template has been created, McMunn specifies preferences and data formats (comma- or tab-delimited) in the Xdata dialog boxes, tells Xdata which file to import via the Xdata menu in XPress…

6. …and clicks Start in the Xdata control panel. McMunn tells us that, depending on the complexity of the data and the speed of the Macintosh being used, Xdata can analyze and format hundreds of records per minute.

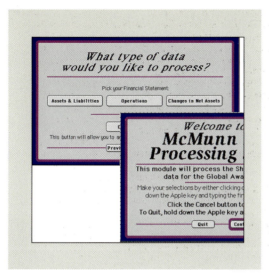

Cleaning up the data

2. Vice President Marty Farlow of McMunn Associates has developed several programs that prepare and massage the raw data before it is run through Xdata.

Stripping out unwanted data

3. Here you can see the results of one of Farlow's data processors as it has been used to strip out unwanted characters and insert formatting flags for Xdata.

Setting up an XPress template

4. Before using Xdata to import the cleaned-up information, McMunn creates an XPress template (above) that includes placeholders for each field in the database.

Australia — 0.8%

News Corp. Limited	44,962	$ 305,162
News Corp. Limited ADR	47,000	2,549,750
Western Mining Corp. Holdings Limited .	482,000	2,883,983
Western Mining Corp. Holdings		
Limited New E 8/94 Shares**	60,250	360,498
		6,099,393

Hong Kong — 3.3%

Champion Technology Holdings . . .	8,948,328	3,265,729
Cheung Kong Holdings	721,300	3,649,907
China Strategic Holdings Limited	3,835,000	2,109,324
FPB Bank Holding Company Limited . .	13,350,400	2,919,914
Henderson Land	798,100	4,637,594
New World Development Company . . .	1,199,549	4,183,752

Formatted and organized data

7. Here you can see some of the sophisticated formatting capabilities of Xdata, including leader dots, tabs and indents, bold headings, vertically aligned numbers, and rules above and below text.

The finished page

8. When combined with Xdata's automatic formatting capabilities, McMunn's typesetting and design background and Farlow's programming expertise form a powerful force in the financial publishing market.

12

How We Produced This Book

Nancy Rice

The front and back covers and the templates for the interior pages of this book were designed in QuarkXPress version 3.2. All production work was performed using QuarkXPress version 3.3. In this chapter, we'll show you how it was done.

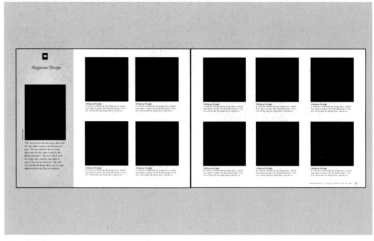

Designing master page templates

1. Rainwater Press commissioned graphic designer Nancy Rice to design the page templates for *Quark Design*. Rice designed two sets of templates: The first, used in this chapter and shown at left, contains wider boxes to show publications that are horizontally oriented, such as the inside pages of a book. The second set of templates, shown above, contains square background boxes to showcase vertically oriented designs such as ads and brochures.

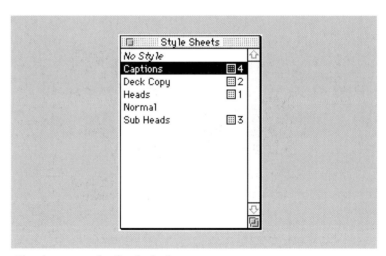

Choosing type styles for the book

4. We chose to use Monotype's Janson and Janson Expert typefaces; we liked Janson's classic look in addition to the flexibility provided by the expert set. The caption text is 9-point Janson with 10 points of leading, while the sub-heads are 10/11 Janson Bold Italic and the caption numbers are 10/10 Janson Expert Bold. The headlines at the beginning of each chapter are 22/24 Janson Italic and the caption text in the chapter opener is 12/14 Janson Italic. The chapter numbers are set in 12-point Futura Extra Bold to complement the page numbers and the folios. Rice set up keyboard shortcuts in the style sheets.

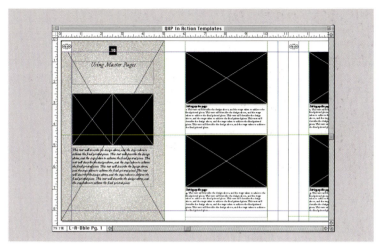

2. Here's a screen shot of one of the master pages, in which you can see all the items that were repeated from page to page: picture boxes, introductory text, captions, chapter number, headline, page guides, and folios.

Creating folios and automatic page numbers

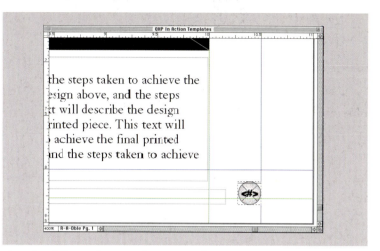

3. Rice set the original folios in 4-point Futura Heavy; we later enlarged them to 5 points. The lefthand folio contains the book title, while the righthand folio changes to reflect the chapter title. For the automatic page numbers, Rice drew a text box, pressed Command 3, and styled the auto page icon in 6-point Futura Extra Bold. The graphic behind the page numbers is a circular text box containing a lavender circular blend that Rice created with the Cool Blends XTension.

Creating blends

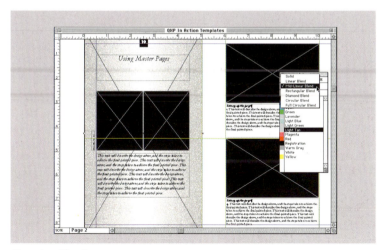

5. To expand on the chapter openers in the previous books of this series, we decided to make use of XPress' automatic blends for the neutral background on the left side of the page. We at first tried the mid-linear blend (shown above), but upon viewing the color proofs, decided it looked off-center. This was due to the fact that the left edge of the picture box that contained the blend extended slightly off the left edge of the page (in order to create a bleed), causing the middle of the blend to appear left-of-center. We then changed the mid-linear blend to a circular blend for a more subtle effect.

Designating colors

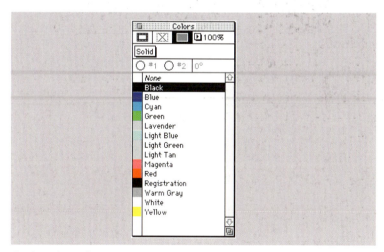

6. Instead of using the same neutral color for all of the background boxes, we devised a palette of four neutral colors that could be used according to the colors of the piece being featured: lavender, light blue, light green, and light tan.

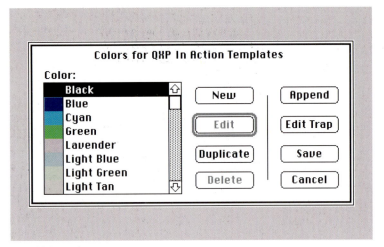

Specifying colors

7. Rice added our custom colors to the QuarkXPress Colors palette via the Edit Colors dialog box, above.

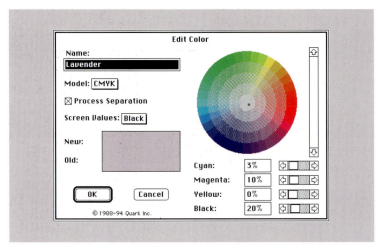

8. Using the CMYK (cyan, magenta, yellow, and black) color model, Rice built our custom colors according to percentages. *Don't forget to check the Process Separation button if you don't want the color to output as a spot color.*

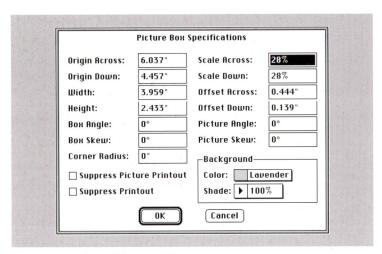

Importing and modifying graphics

11. We imported TIFF files and other graphics using XPress' Get Picture command and modified their size via the Scale Across and Scale Down fields in the Picture Box Specifications dialog (Modify command under the Item menu). We also adjusted the size of our graphics via the X and Y percentages in the Measurements palette. Most of our screen shots appear at either 22% or 28% their original size. The RGB TIFF images were converted to CMYK format using PhotoFlash and an AppleScript to automate the process.

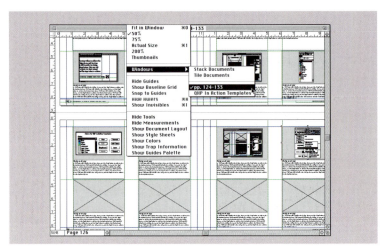

Navigating XPress documents

12. While creating each chapter, we usually had several XPress files open at once: the original XPress document sent to us by the designer, a working version of the original document created with the Save As command, and the XPress document containing the actual chapter. We moved from one document to another using the Windows submenu (under the View menu), which provided us with a list of all open documents from which to choose.

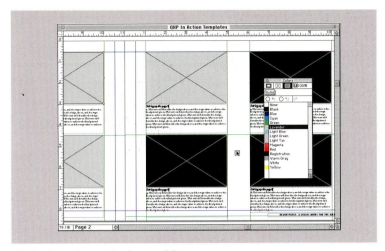

Assigning colors to background boxes

9. Before importing screen shots and other graphic images into each chapter, we colored the background boxes by clicking on one of the four custom colors in the Colors palette and dragging it on top of the picture box.

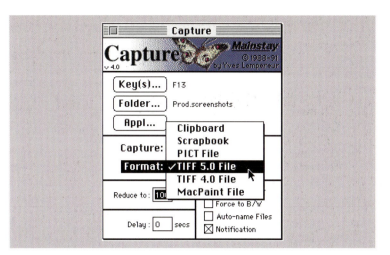

Taking screen captures

10. In order to depict a work in progress or to display dialog boxes, palettes, and any other on-screen information, we took pictures of the XPress files using Capture from Mainstay. Unlike other screen capture programs which save screenshots in PICT format, Capture allowed us to save our files in TIFF format. TIFF files tend to be much less problematic than PICT files at output time.

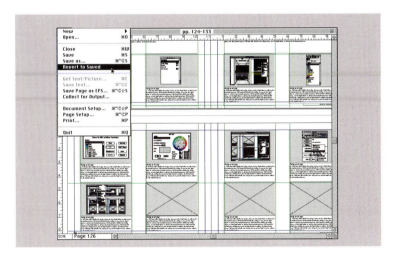

Reverting to last saved version

13. We relied heavily on XPress' Revert to Saved option (under the File menu), which allowed us to modify the working version of a designer's files (without saving those modifications) and to then revert back to the original version of the file once we were done poking around. We always maintained at least one backup of the original file—just in case.

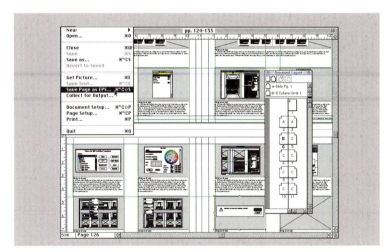

Saving XPress pages as EPS (Encapsulated PostScript) images

14. In order to display a high-resolution version of the XPress documents we showcased, we used the Save Page as EPS command under the File menu (Command Option Shift S), making sure that the correct page was highlighted in the Document Layout palette. *EPS files cannot be edited, so it's important to save the original document in case you decide to make changes.*

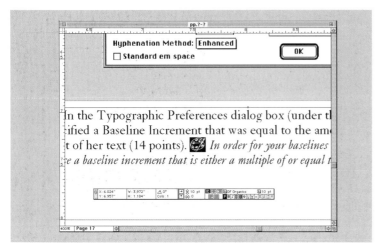

15. Here's the Save Page as EPS dialog box, which allows you to name the file, select a location, scale the image, and select a format (Mac color, Mac black and white, DCS, PC color, and so on), among other things. *When you send a QuarkXPress file that contains EPS images to a printer or imagesetter, you still need to include the fonts and graphics included in that image for the pages to output properly.*

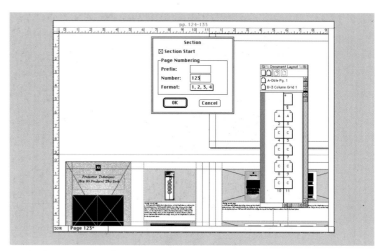

Assigning page numbers

16. Although we used the auto page numbering feature in our master pages, we still needed to tell XPress where to begin the numbering for each new chapter, which was created as a separate QuarkXPress document. With the first page of the document selected in the Document Layout palette, we chose Section from the Page menu, clicked the Section Start button, and inserted a page number. This dialog also let us select our numbering format, such as roman numerals, digits, or letters. *The first page of each section is marked with an asterisk in the Document Layout palette and in the current page number field.*

Creating icons

19. To signify technical tips and design hints within our captions, we used the icons of a magnifying glass and a painter's palette from the Organics collection of Letraset's Fontek DesignFonts. These graphic images are actually in font format, so we could type them in and size them just as if we were setting type. We set the "picture fonts" slightly larger than the text at 10 points.

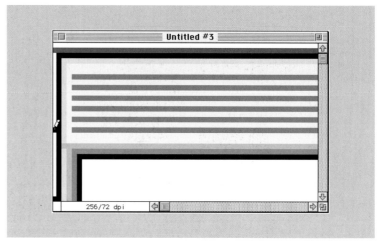

Cleaning up screen shots

20. Although Capture allowed us a certain amount of precision in selecting the area of the screen we wanted to show, many of our screen shots needed cleaning up in a bitmap program. We used Electronic Arts' Studio/32 to smooth out the rough edges, as seen in the above closeup of a screen capture.

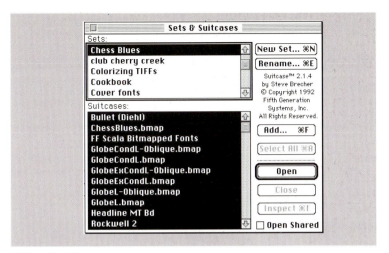

Managing fonts

17. With each new XPress document featured in the book came an entirely new set of fonts. We managed the hundreds of fonts shown in the pages of this book using the font utility Suitcase II, which allowed us to establish sets of typefaces for each chapter, opening them only when necessary.

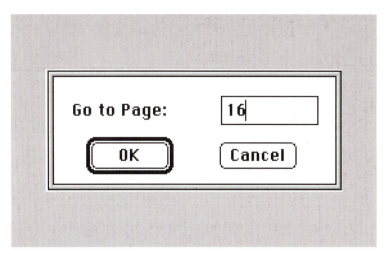

Moving from page to page

18. When moving from one page to another, we found XPress' Go to Page feature handier than double-clicking page icons in the Document Layout palette. Simply press Command J, enter the page number you want to go to, and hit Return.

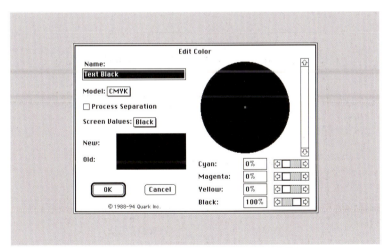

Preparing films for translations

21. Because this book would be translated into many languages, we output five separations with two black films. All captions, subheads, chapter titles, intro text, folios, and black-and-white dialog boxes were assigned a fifth spot color, called Text Black, so that they could be translated. The remaining color art and dialog boxes were separated via the normal CMYK plates, with translations for color dialog boxes manually stripped in. The printer then stripped together the two black films for each different edition of this book.

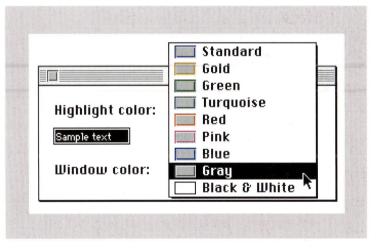

Adjusting on-screen colors

22. To keep our black-and-white screen shots free of color so that they would appear entirely on the fifth (Text Black) printing plate used for foreign-language editions of this book, we used the Macintosh Color Control Panel device to select a black-and-white highlight color and a gray window color. Although it may not look like it, the standard windows on your Macintosh screen contain just the tiniest amount of blue, which will show up on your cyan printing plate if not eliminated.

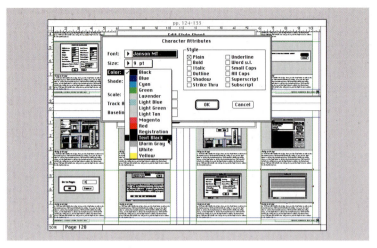

23. The Text Black color was assigned to all text except page numbers and artist bylines (which would not be translated) via the Character Attributes dialog box (from the Edit Style sheets dialog).

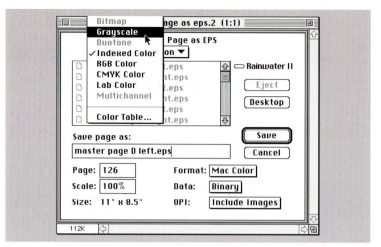

Assigning graphics to a fifth plate
24. Assigning black-and-white dialog boxes to the fifth plate was a little more tricky. We first opened the TIFF image in Adobe Photoshop and saved it as a grayscale TIFF, ensuring that any unwanted color information was eliminated.

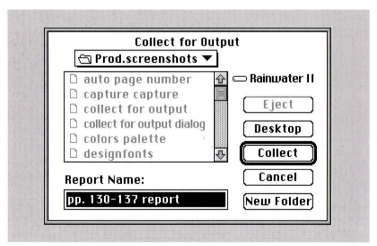

27. Here's the Collect for Output dialog for this chapter. XPress automatically names the report for you, but you can change it to something else if you want. This dialog box also lets you choose the destination or create a new folder for the collected graphics.

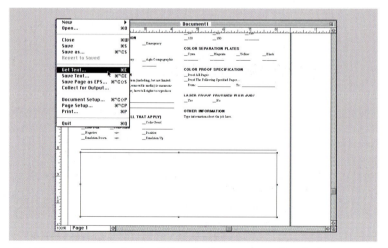

28. Although you can print the Collect for Output report directly from a word processing program, you can also import the text into the Output Request template provided with QuarkXPress. Simply open the template, perform a Save As with a new name, select the text box at the bottom of the template, select Get Text from the File menu (Command E)…

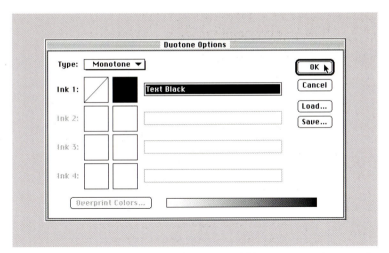

25. The grayscale TIFF image was then converted to a monotone image and assigned the Text Black color from the Duotone Options dialog box (above) while still in Adobe Photoshop. That image was saved as an EPS image, which would then be used in our final QuarkXPress document to be output on the Text Black plate along with all the text.

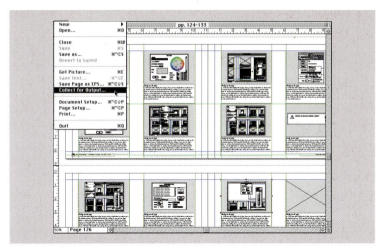

Sending files to a service bureau
26. Before sending our QuarkXPress files to the service bureau (this book takes up a whopping 800MB contained on 4 200MB SyQuest cartridges), we performed a Collect for Output (under the File menu) on each QuarkXPress file to make sure the necessary fonts and graphics were included with each document.

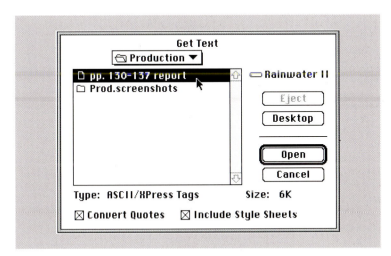

29. …select and open the appropriate output report…

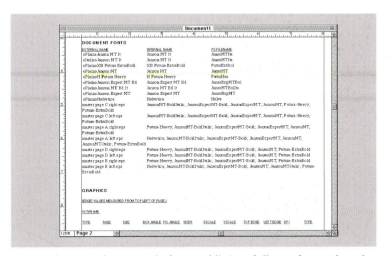

30. …and now you have a neatly formatted listing of all your fonts and graphics, as well as system and application information, to give to your service bureau along with the files to be output. *Make sure that the Include Style Sheets button is checked when importing the report to retain formatting.*

Contributors

Gretchen Achilles
Doubleday
1540 Broadway
New York, NY 10036 USA
(212) 354-6500 phone
(212) 302-7985 facsimile

Kristy Lantz Astry
The Buddy System
P.O. Box 62051
Littleton, CO 80162 USA
(303) 978-0946 phone

Fabien Baron
Hearst Magazines
224 West 57th Street
New York, NY 10019 USA
(212) 903-5064 phone
(212) 581-4803 facsimile

Arlene Boyer
Barnhart Advertising
455 Sherman Street, #500
Denver, CO 80203 USA
(303) 698-3200 phone
(303) 777-8712 facsimile

Jeff Cheney
14 Horatio Street, #7J
New York, NY 10014 USA
(212) 924-9624 phone
74250,3034 CompuServe
jcheney@netcom.com Internet

Michael Diehl
Michael Diehl Design
1415 Norton
Glendale, CA 91202 USA
(818) 552-4110 phone
(818) 552-4111 facsimile

Kristin FitzGerrell
Kristin FitzGerrell Graphic Design
2432 10th Street
Boulder, CO 80304 USA
(303) 447-0929 phone
(303) 3447-9839 facsimile

Kevin P. Hambel
IHS Publishing Group
17730 West Peterson Road
P.O. Box 159
Libertyville, IL 60048 USA
(708) 362-8711 phone
(708) 362-3484 facsimile

David High
High Design
305 Lake Shore Drive West
Putnam Valley, NY 10579 USA
(914) 528-7950 phone
(914) 528-0366 facsimile

Eric Jacobs
The Daily Pennsylvanian
4015 Walnut Street
Philadelphia, PA 19104 USA
(215) 898-6581 phone
(215) 898-2050 facsimile

Donna Lehner
Lehner & Whyte Graphic Design
8-10 South Fullerton Avenue
Montclair, NJ 07042 USA
(201) 746-1335 phone
(201) 746-0178 facsimile

Dermot Mac Cormack
Marcolina Design Inc.
1100 E. Hector Street, Suite 335
Conshohocken, PA 19428 USA
(610) 940-0680 phone
(610) 940-0638 facsimile

Dan Marcolina
Marcolina Design Inc.
1100 E. Hector Street, Suite 335
Conshohocken, PA 19428 USA
(610) 940-0680 phone
(610) 940-0638 facsimile

Larry McMunn
McMunn Associates
900 Haddon Avenue, Suite 436
Collingswood, NJ 08108 USA
(609) 858-3440 phone
(609) 858-5117 facsimile

Rainwater Press
6737 East Fifth Avenue
Denver, CO 80220 USA
(303) 377-1966 phone
(303) 377-9424 facsimile
76702,1136 CompuServe

Edward Renaud
Graphor Consultation
682 rue William
Montreal, Quebec H3C 1N9 Canada
(514) 875-4500 phone
(514) 875-1014 facsimile

St. Remy Press
682 rue William
Montreal, Quebec H3C 1N9 Canada
871-9696 phone
871-2230 facsimile

NancyRice
Nancy Rice Graphic Design
1738 Blake Street
Denver, CO 80202 USA
(303) 295-0464 phone
(303) 295-9596 facsimile

Michael Smilanic
Barnhart Advertising
455 Sherman Street, #500
Denver, CO 80203 USA
(303) 698-3200 phone
(303) 777-8712 facsimile

Hugh Whyte
Lehner & Whyte Graphic Design
8-10 South Fullerton Avenue
Montclair, NJ 07042 USA
(201) 746-1335 phone
(201) 746-0178 facsimile

Vendors

Letraset USA
40 Eisenhower Drive
Paramus, NJ 07653 USA
(201) 845-6100 phone
(201) 845-5047 facsimile

Managing Editor Software
101 Greenwood Avenue, Suite 550
Jenkintown, PA 19046 USA
(215) 886-5662 phone
(215) 886-5681 facsimile

North Atlantic Publishing Systems
Nine Acton Road, Suite 13
Chelmsford, MA 01824 USA
(508) 250-8080 phone
(508) 250-8179 facsimile

Quark Inc.
1800 Grant Street
Denver, CO 80206 USA
(303) 894-8888 phone
(303) 894-3399 facsimile

Quark Systems Ltd.
20 Quarry Street
Guildford
Surrey GU1 3UY UK
(44) 483-453-011

Quark Japan
Room 201, 2-1-12 Mita
Meguro-ku, Tokyo 153 Japan
(03) 3716-7221 phone
(03) 3716-7147 facsimile

XChange
P.O. Box 270578
Fort Collins, CO 80527 USA
(303) 229-0620 phone
(303) 229-9773 facsimile

XChange International
1-2 Bromley Place
London W1P 5HB UK
(44) 071-637-2966 phone
(44) 071-637-2842 facsimile

Index

About the Author

Dan Bettinger

Nancy McCarthy owns Rainwater Press, an editorial services and book packaging firm in Denver, Colorado. She is the editor of several books, including *News by Design, Camera Ready With QuarkXPress, So You Wanna Buy A Mac,* and the *Thomas Munroe Color Reference Manual.* Nancy also writes articles on electronic publishing technology for *Step-by-Step Electronic Design, Publish, MacWEEK,* and *Technique,* in addition to writing advertising copy and speaking at seminars on topics relevant to electronic publishers.

A former managing editor of *Personal Publishing* magazine, she also managed the editorial staff of Quark Inc.'s Creative Services department, where she was responsible for the company's marketing and sales publications. Before her career in the electronic publishing industry, Nancy was the editor of a weekly magazine in Okinawa, Japan. She holds a Bachelor of Science degree in Advertising from the University of Illinois.

Among her non-computer related accomplishments, Nancy has written an unpublished novel about her experiences living in Japan, studied Japanese language skills at the University of Maryland in Okinawa, and taught classical piano to 25 children and adults. When not writing, editing, or answering e-mail at her computer, Nancy spends time with her husband and two young sons, plays the piano, reads Anne Rice novels, shops by catalog, and talks on the phone.